Celebrating our Raw Nature

REVISED

RECIPES FOR PLANT-BASED LIVING CUISINE

with

Dorit

Certified Living Foods Chef and Chopra Centre Educator

Book Publishing Company
Summertown, Tennessee

Published in the United States by
Book Publishing Company
P.O. Box 99
Summertown, TN 38483
1-888-260-8458

Printed in Canada

ISBN 978-1-57067-208-8

15 14 13 12 11 10 09 08 07   9 8 7 6 5 4 3 2 1

Celebrating our raw nature : recipes for plant-based, living cuisine / with Dorit — revised
    p. cm.
  Includes index.
  ISBN 978-1-57067-208-8
1. Vegetarian cookery. 2. Raw foods.

TX837.C37 2007
641.5'636--dc22

                                    2007021632

We are a member of Green Press Initiative. We have elected to print this title on paper with post-consumer recycled content and processed chlorine free, which saved the following natural resources:

67 trees   46 million BTUs
3,120 lbs of solid waste   5,854 lbs of greenhouse   green
24,299 gallons of water   gases   press
                                                          INITIATIVE

For more information visit: www.greenpressinitiative.org. Savings calculations thanks to the Environmental Defense Paper Calculator at www.papercalculator.org

Contents

Acknowledgments

This book is the sum total of much love and a wide network of support. There are just too many people to list here by name, so I wish to express my deepest appreciation and gratitude to all my former clients in New York and Toronto who have so encouraged and supported my work from the very beginning.

For Barbara Mitchell Haggerty, Phyllis Dilea, Roberta Roll, Carlene Toole, Joyce de Marzi, Barbara Haines, and Bozena Wysocki, whose love and devotion stand out like huge flames burning so brightly that I feel so blessed and honored to have had them stay present for me and to call them friends. For Ayala Biran, Ayala Katz, Mary Danelski, Schmuel Vlodinger, and Eva Getz, all still in Israel, who have contributed to my life in such profound ways that I wonder how I would have navigated my life to a place of sanity without them. I gratefully acknowledge Ron Kato for all his love and unfailing support, and wish to thank Ron Gilmore for having "come to my rescue" during numerous technical challenges with the computer, and without whom this book would probably still be lost in cyberspace.

Lastly, I dedicate this book and all my love to Gita Katz, who is actually my inspiration for writing this and whose spirit follows me every time I am in the kitchen creating yet another concoction. For Rami Katz who shares the spirit realm with Gita now, and who I loved more than I thought it possible to love any being on earth. To my fleet of family scattered throughout Canada, and especially Britany and Tiffany, who are treasures in my heart, I thank you all.

—Dorit

Recipe Credits

The following recipes were contributed by the generous individuals or sites listed. My gratitude to all of them.

Contributor: Antje and Roman, www.GenefitNutrition.com

Cocomango Chutney (page 162)
Coconut Kefir (page 158)
Custardy Durian Spread (page 103)
Gary's Green Smoothie (page 56)

Contributor: Thammarath Touch Jamikorn, www.rawganique.com

Hemp Pesto (page 151)
Peppery Hempfredo Touch Al Dente (page 137)
Stir-Frei (Be Free!) Pad Thai (page 141)
Zucchi-Ghetti with Marinara Sauce (page 145)

Contributor: kristo@4Vibrance.com

Cheezy Tortilla Rolls (page 116)
Hearty Seed Porridge (page 25)
Quinoa Delight (page 137)
Super Sprout Spread (page 164)
Thai Coconut Curry (page 143)
Thai Goddess Dressing (page 80)

Contributor: Ron Gilmore, www.uncooking-show.com

Sweet-and-Spicy Brown Rice (page 120)

Foreword

Dorit is a breath of fresh air. She brings to us the gift of mindfulness. She reminds us of who we are, why we're here, and how it all relates to the quality of the foods we put into our bodies. Her philosophy of food is not primarily about the vitamins or calories or antioxidants, but rather about our relationship to it—how we connect to it, our state of being when we consume it, and our intentions behind eating it.

Dorit's wonderful perspective comes directly from her own multicultural, spiritual background. She comes to us from France, Israel, Ireland, and Canada; from being a yogi and a meditator, a chef and a workshop leader, a counselor and a movement therapist. Anyone who spends time with Dorit at her workshops and food demos knows well her enthusiasm for teaching. But that is merely an outgrowth of a more primary mission—the desire to help us find ourselves. And that is ultimately how she teaches self-healing. Yes, she delivers recipes and techniques, but more importantly, she imparts her personal guidance, love, and inspiration in every class.

If that's not satisfying enough, then we eat! She may start with live granola, or coconut seaweed soup, then on to Bombay curry, jicama with mushroom gravy, sushi chips, and finally vegan ice cream, nut nog, and energizer cookies. The recipes flow like the colorful brush strokes of a skilled artist. To the uninitiated, this raw vegan diet appears limited. In truth, the plant kingdom offers a nearly endless variety of nutritious choices. Once you cleanse your palate of salt, MSG, sugar, and preservatives, the taste sensations you'll discover will make you feel like Marco Polo stumbling upon new civilizations.

You are holding a virtual workshop in your hands. Are you ready for a dietary makeover? If you're docked in the doldrums of the standard American diet, if you've gone rudderless on the cosmic smorgasbord of life, if you're stuck in the lard of addictive patterns and would rather be overjoyed than overweight, then buckle your seat belt and blast off with your copy of *Celebrating our Raw Nature*. The cure is in the kitchen, and you won't find a more devoted captain than the indefatigable Dorit.

—*Steve Meyerowitz, "Sproutman"*

Steve Meyerowitz is a health crusader and author of eight books including *Juice Fasting & Detoxification, Wheatgrass: Nature's Finest Medicine,* and *Power Juices Super Drinks.* You can visit him at www.Sproutman.com.

*I*ntroduction

*T*he Art of Raw and the Sacred Act of Eating

Being "raw " involves a consistent practice of living with, by, and for the laws of nature and the wisdom that arises from our intuitive faculties, and observing and studying the effects of this lifestyle. Because food comes from nature, we keep it as close to its natural form as possible. Food is also seasonal and regional, so we aim to eat the foods that are grown in our own geographic locations, according to the seasons.

When we observe animals in the wild, we see that they eat only when they are hungry. They seem to intuitively know which foods are intended for their digestive tract and how much of them to eat. In practicing the "art of raw," we do likewise.

If there are times while practicing the art of raw that we find ourselves eating a slice of whole grain bread or cooked soup in the depths of a chilly winter frost, we refrain from condemning ourselves or others. Instead, we practice acceptance and gratitude, and eat the cooked food mindfully and with enjoyment, perhaps adding some raw sprouts, green leaves, or E3Live (an organic freshwater plant algae) to the dish. Usually, though, most people who practice long enough find themselves enjoying a completely uncooked vegan meal on a winter's night without even being aware that the weather is cold and damp. Cravings disappear, and we simply enjoy what nature has in store for us. At that point, we will know we have mastered the art of raw.

Once you change your relationship with food, you will discover that you no longer need to resort to restrictive dieting, worrying about how much you weigh, or thinking of your body as "the enemy." There is no enemy. When we change our habits so that we fully participate in our day-to-day food choices and the functioning of our bodies, we will make conscious decisions that allow us to actively take care of our precious bodies. Your desire for harmful food and activities will dissipate, and your yearning for wholesome, raw, natural food and health-promoting activities will increase. You will learn to listen to your body and make choices in response to your physical needs and demands. Since I have been on a raw vegan diet, I have become a voracious seasonal eater. The only desire that remains constant throughout the seasons is my craving for avocados, and even that wanes from time to time.

Be a Conscious Eater

When practicing the art of raw, there are two essential guidelines for how to eat. First, eat instinctively. The well-attuned body knows what to eat, when to eat, and when to stop eating. Second, when you eat, engage all your senses.

It is important to make sure that we include food of varying sizes, shapes, and textures, and that we take time to touch it before we prepare it. Our sense of smell contributes to our enjoyment of life and also alerts us to unsafe conditions (such as when food is spoiled). When we breathe in the aroma of a ripe, juicy mango or tangerine, our saliva starts flowing even before the food touches our lips. This is the very beginning of the digestive process.

Our sense of taste help us select and take pleasure in our food. Our sense of sight helps us learn about and appreciate color. Color has the ability to stimulate or calm our other senses and affect our mood. It's one of the reasons I recommend blue as the dominant color with which to set a table if a client tends to overeat.

Eat according to what I call the "rotation method." Simply put, this entails rotating what, when, and how you eat. The first guideline is to eat mindfully, as this is the foundation for the sacred art of eating. You will gain so much if you just eat with awareness that all the other principles of the rotation method will simply fall into place. The next guideline is to eat a wide variety of foods—rotate an assortment of types, colors, textures, shapes, and aromas.

The mood we are in when we are eating is crucial to how our bodies respond to our food. If we are angry, anxious, restless, or are experiencing other emotions that affect our nervous system, some of the nutrients in our food may be lost as a result of the smooth flow of energy for digestion being obstructed. This can also happen if we eat standing up, when we are in a hurry, or when we are distracted by other activities (talking, writing, reading, watching television, and so forth). When you eat, keep your attention focused on your food, and develop a sense of gratitude for the farmers, sun, earth, rain, and life-force energies that combined to create it.

A Word about Food Combining

"Food combining" entails eating foods that are compatible with each other in terms of digestive chemistry. Many people experience digestive orders of all kinds, including indigestion, heartburn, reflux, gas, and bloating. If you are among those who have such symptoms, you might find it valuable to experiment with these principles. Food combining can be especially beneficial for people who have digestive disorders, cancer, or autoimmune disorders such as HIV, AIDS, or lupus.

Pay attention to what food your body wants, how much it wants, when it wants it, and the form of food it wants (such as liquid, semisoft, or solid food). If you want to learn about food combining, get a book dedicated to this subject or work with an experienced teacher or nutritionist who follows these principles.

All the recipes in this book call for only raw, fresh, wild-crafted, and/or organic ingredients. If fresh fruit is not available, then by all means use the dried form. You will, however, sometimes need to soak dried fruit in advance. Occasionally, in the ingredient lists for the recipes, I reiterate "raw," especially when referring to nuts, seeds, and items that you might be buying packaged, such as oil, olives, or capers. This is done as a reminder to those of you who are new to this lifestyle; it does not mean that the other ingredients are not raw too!

Because most of the recipes here have leafy greens as the main component, if you are following food combining guidelines, they ought to work for you. If they do not, then just omit the ingredient that you would prefer not to use.

Raw On a Budget

I have heard many excuses for why someone doesn't want to try raw living. At the top of the list is that it is too expensive. For those on a tight budget, every penny spent ought to be for the most beneficial and nutrient-dense food possible. It is possible to eat a variety of nutritious raw food while sticking to a monthly budget.

In addition to basic supplies, augment your diet by purchasing a few specialty items. Here's an example of items you could purchase each month:
• January : three or four bottles of E3Live
• February: one bottle of sprouted flax-hemp-maca powder
• March: one bottle each raw hemp oil and raw coconut oil
• April: Celtic sea salt and camu camu powder
• May: Himalayan sea salt, mulberries, and Incan berries
• June :Nama Shoyu and umeboshi vinegar
• July: sea vegetables in bulk
• August: raw pumpkin seed butter and raw almond butter
• September: wild rice and raw black sesame paste
and so on.

Also, buy seasonally as you will get the best bargains. Another way is to buy in bulk, or better yet, form a buying club or join a raw food support group that has discounts from companies that sell what you are looking for. Frequent farmers' markets when you are not able to go foraging for wild plants, and when possible, visit a farm or volunteer to work on one in exchange for fresh produce.

Calling All Children to the Kitchen!

Children are so at home in nature, and when it comes to a raw vegan lifestyle, there is much that we can learn from them. Encourage children to experiment and use their sense of touch rather than trying to teach them kitchen basics, such as knife skills. In fact, I believe that all knives ought to be put away when children are in the kitchen. Instead of using tools and equipment, teach them (or better yet, let them teach you) how to squeeze and twist produce for juicing, and tear leafy vegetables as an alternative to cutting them. Let children assist you with picking out their own aprons and clean-up supplies. Encourage them to have their own little area in the kitchen and to paint or draw their names there, and keep all sanitation and safety instructions right there at their eye level. You might need to get a special stool or table for them, as well as a washing bowl and towel so they can wash their hands frequently to avoid cross-contamination. Teaching food safety to children when they are young means simply showing them how to use a vegetable brush and clean running water to wash fruits and vegetables, and helping them understand the importance of clean hands and fingernails.

If children are mature and aware enough to use equipment, please make sure that you or another alert adult is supervising them at all times.

Children often respond strongly to food and may go through phases when they will eat only items that have a certain color, texture, or smell. Do not be alarmed. One of my private clients (a medical doctor) was a bit hesitant and expressed her concern to me when her toddler was refusing to eat anything but bread and red bell peppers. I assured her that children eat instinctively, and that when her little body was ready for other forms of nutrients, her daughter would move on to them. This indeed was exactly what she eventually did. I had another client who panicked when her little boy would eat only fruits. I pointed out to her that we were in the middle of a particularly hot and humid Southern California summer, and wasn't she craving these fruits as well? Her reply was that of course she was, but in order to maintain a balanced diet, she was forcing herself to have a little bit of other foods as well. I asked her if her son was suffering from lethargy or having a rough time with the heat and humidity. She replied, "No. That is what is so strange." I then asked her the same question of herself, to which she replied, "Of course I am, isn't everybody?" I pointed out that she had just told me that her son was not "suffering," had lots of energy, and was doing well. I also acknowledged that although I do not like heat, I was tolerating it very well, and that like her son, I had given in to my instincts for moisture-laden, cooling fruits only.

Learn what works for your children at mealtimes; to do so, make space and time for them in the kitchen and at farmers' markets and farms where they can pick their own fruit and vegetables. The more involved they are with growing, picking, and sprouting their own food, the more healthful their eating habits will be. One of my favorite gifts to give children is sprouting jars and other sprouting equipment. I have also suggested to clients seeking to raise healthier families that the fun of sprouting be assigned to a different child each month. It is such a joy to watch the delight they have when they master this learning tool. It does wonders for their self-confidence, especially when the entire family gathers around before mealtime to watch and celebrate as that child harvests the sprouts for the meal.

Children seem to naturally understand food combining. They simply do not like to have a lot of ingredients at any given meal. So please do not call your children "fussy eaters." They are simply respecting the rules of food combining, and their digestion, assimilation, and elimination will be a lot better for it. If your child is okay with eating what I call "macro meals" (several ingredients mixed together to form one dish), then they will enjoy the recipes offered in this book. If, like me, they prefer "micro meals," allow them to alter whatever they wish to in the recipes.

The Raw, Vegan, Green Kitchen

I would like to see a study done on the positive environmental impact of a raw vegan lifestyle. I am personally dedicated to restoring the integrity of our land, air, and water by building and encouraging others to create more "green," raw, vegan, living-food kitchens across the globe. Remember, there was a time when we did not even have kitchens; we simply picked our meals straight from the trees and any residue went right back to the land. Some of us can still do that, depending on where we live. For the rest, here are some suggestions to help us become aware of the repercussions of every decision we make.

Every time we run appliances at home and keep our houses lit, warm, and cool, we cause carbon dioxide to be emitted, which traps heat in the atmosphere. How can a raw vegan lifestyle help to prevent or diminish this? Think about the effect of every stove and oven that is being turned on to cook a meal, even as you are reading this!. A raw, vegan, eco-friendly kitchen is part of the solution, especially if we use available resources, such as rainwater, and seek out other ways to reduce our dependence on fossil fuels and nonrenewable resources. Our awareness can contribute to the development of new technologies and alternative energy that reduce carbon dioxide emissions. This consciousness can also guide us when we construct or furnish our kitchens, whether they are at home or in commercial facilities. If we are going to be raw and vegan, the least we can do is consider the impact that our food preparation space has on the environment.

I trust that you will be inspired by the information and recipes you find in this book. Please join me on the road to freedom and health as we celebrate our raw nature together.

Dorit
www.serenityspaces.org

Glossary

Algorroba (*Prosopis juliflora*), known in most English-speaking countries as mesquite, is a leguminous plant found in South America that was spread to arid zones around the world, including southwestern United States. Mesquite powder is made from the entire mesquite pod, which is ground. It includes the protein-rich seed and produces a meal that is highly nutritious. Raw, wild-crafted mesquite pod meal is rich in calcium, magnesium, potassium, iron, and zinc.

Agave nectar/syrup is produced from *Agave salmiana*, a plant native to southwestern United States. During the processing of raw agave nectar, the temperature ideally never exceeds 115 degrees F. This minimal processing and minimal heat retains vitamins, minerals, and enzymes that are not found in other processed sweeteners It can be most useful for people who are diabetic and have insulin resistance (syndrome X). This is because agave has a relatively low glycemic index due to its higher proportion of fructose and low level of glucose.

Camu camu (*Myrciaria dubia*), also known as cacari and camocamo, has the highest recorded amount of natural vitamin C of any plant known. It also has a full complement of minerals and amino acids that can aid in the absorption of vitamin C. In most Western countries, it is only available as a powdered extract. It is traditionally used to strengthen the immune system, balance mood, support healthy blood, improve energy and vitality, and promote a healthy heart.

Celtic sea salt (also called Celtic sea minerals) are natural sea salts obtained by evaporation of sea water and produced without refining, oven drying, or chemical additives. Naturally sun-dried sea salt is charged with energy. These charged minerals go right to where they are most needed in the body, unlike the bleached and refined table salt that is so prevalent and devoid of health-promoting minerals.

Cherimoyas grow on a tree that is often referred to as the "ice cream tree," and the fruit is well worth waiting for until it is in season. Cherimoyas are heart-shaped fruit with green skin. The flesh is white and contains black pits. Most cherimoyas ripen within two to three days at room temperature. When they are ripe, they become greenish-black on the outside and give to slight pressure, like an avocado or peach.

Dates are high in dietary fiber, carbohydrates, potassium, and vitamins A_1, B_2, B_3, and B_5, and contain more than twenty different amino acids. These acids help us digest and assimilate carbohydrates more easily and control blood sugar levels and fatty acids in the body.

Durian, named for an Indonesian word meaning "thorny," resembles an unripe coconut with spines covering its thick, green rind. The most popular and expensive brand of durian in Thailand is called "Morn Tong." Known for the intensity of its smell, some describe durian's aroma as foul, although it is prized in Southeast Asia and by many in the vegan, raw community as the "king of fruits."

E3Live and E3AFA are products that are available from Vision Inc. The names stand for *Aphanizomenon flos-aquae* (AFA), which means "invisible flower of the water." They are both made from a fresh water nutritional plant known as cyanophyta, which grows in nearly all droplets of sunlit water and in every gram of soil, on the bark of trees and the surfaces of rocks. E3AFA is the Refractance-Window dried crystal flake form of the AFA, which comes as either vegetarian capsules or loose powderlike crystal flakes. Both are excellent foods. The liquid form of E3Live is closest to its natural high-energy state found in nature and is the ideal way to consume AFA. E3AFA will further boost your nutritional intake; it is also convenient to use when at work and while traveling, if refrigeration is not available.

E3 with Phenalmin is a new formula from Vision Inc, the company that harvests E3Live from Lake Klamath. This is a fresh-frozen green algae known as *Aphanizomenon flos-aquae* (AFA). It contains 500 percent more chlorophyll than wheatgrass and has high levels of Phenalmin, which is also found in chocolate.

Germinated brown rice is simply brown rice soaked in water until it just begins to bud. The outer bran layer becomes soft and is better able to absorb water, making it easier for us to eat it raw. Rice (like most seeds, nuts, and other grains) reaches its nutritional peak during germination. This process activates dormant enzymes, increasing the amount of digestible vitamins, minerals, amino acids, and other nutrients.

Himalayan salt is made from crystal stones that come from one specific location in the Himalayan Mountains of Pakistan This salt is hand crushed and very pale pink.

Incan berries are also known as cape gooseberries and goldenberries in English-speaking countries. In other parts of the world, particularly in South America, this fruit is known as agauaymanto berry, mullaca, uvilla, or uchuva. The dried Incan berry looks like a yellow-orange raisin and has a tart sweet-and-sour flavor. They are known for their antihistamine, antiviral, anticarcinogenic, and anti-inflammatory properties, and are high in phosphorous, vitamins A, C, B_1, B_2, B_6, and B_{12}. They also bear the distinction of being 16 percent protein, which is extremely high for a fruit.

Kuzu root is a very popular medicine in Japan and China. It is used in two ways: as powdered starch and as whole dried root. Some experts in Japan and China use it to treat colds and minor aches and pains. Eating lots of foods made with kuzu starch can have the same effects, and doing so is considered good preventive medicine.

Lucuma is a delicately flavored tropical fruit, native to the cool highlands of South America and very popular in Peru. In North America, it is mainly available dehydrated as lucuma flour or powder; it is typically used for making ice creams and puddings.

Mulberry (*Morus*) is a genus of ten to sixteen species that are native to warm, temperate, and subtropical regions. Ripe mulberries may help with anemia, constipation, insomnia, irritability, tinnitus, diabetes, vertigo, premature graying, dry cough, excessive thirst, paralysis, and stomach ulcers. Mulberries are also known to support the liver, kidneys, joints, and circulatory system. Unripe mulberries can be toxic and should not be eaten.

Nama Shoyu is raw, organic, unpasteurized soy sauce. It is aged for four years in cedar kegs by a unique double-brew process, so it can be made with less salt while retaining its full-bodied flavor and delicate bouquet. It is rich in living enzymes and other beneficial organisms.

Palm nectar is a well-known delicacy in Thailand and the South Pacific. It is an extremely sweet and delicious beverage. Make sure you choose unpasteurized palm nectar with no preservatives or chemicals. After a few days left at ambient temperature, palm nectar transforms into a naturally bubbly champagne.

Rapadura is pure dried sugarcane juice that has been granulated. It is rich in iron and is a more nutritious alternative to sugar.

Raspberries are high in dietary fiber and are a great source of vitamin C and folic acid. Although the most common variety is the red raspberry, others can be found in a range of colors: yellow, orange, amber, white, and black. Raspberries are best stored in the refrigerator for up to three days. Keep them as dry as possible, as any type of moisture hastens their decay.

Strawberries do not ripen after they are picked, so make sure you choose plump, brightly colored berries with fresh green caps. If you will not be consuming them soon, store the unwashed, unhulled berries in a covered container in the refrigerator. Fresh strawberries are loaded with phytonutrients that promote health. They also contain potent antioxidants that have repeatedly been shown to help protect cell structures in the body and prevent oxygen damage in all of the body's organ systems. The unique phenol content of strawberries is why they are often recommended as a heart-protective, anticancer, and anti-inflammatory fruit.

Umeboshi vinegar (and the plum from which it is made) have a long-standing reputation in Japan as the "king of alkaline foods." It is an extremely flavorful addition to sauces. Umeboshi vinegar is produced in

Japan and is a salty, sour liquid that is a by-product of making umeboshi (pickled umeboshi plums), which are actually Japanese apricots. Technically, this product is not a true vinegar. I have included it in some of the recipes in this book as a digestive aid for those who might have trouble tolerating highly cruciferous vegetables, and because of its reputed antibacterial qualities.

Vitamineral Green is the brand name for a raw, organic, green superfood powder that is loaded with nutrient-dense ingredients like barley, wheatgrass, alfalfa, kamut grass, green vegetables, algae, sea vegetables, and enzymes. It is readily absorbed and truly effective. Simply add one to three tablespoons to fresh juice or water and shake it well to dissolve it.

Yacon (*Smallanthus sonchifolius*) is a distant relative of the sunflower, with edible tubers and leaves. The syrup is a naturally sweet treat and is possibly the world's richest source of fructooligosaccharide (FOS), a unique type of sugar that cannot be absorbed by the body. Because the sugar in yacon is mostly FOS, the syrup is low in calories. It is a glucose-free sweetener that is suitable for diabetics and others who want to reduce sugar intake yet still want to eat desserts. Yacon syrup works amazingly well as a sweetener for raw cakes, cookies, and ice cream. FOS also acts as a prebiotic, serving as food for the "friendly" bacteria in the colon, and includes *Lactobacillus* and *Bifido* bacteria. It provides health benefits, including aiding digestion and enhancing the absorption of calcium and magnesium. Like most raw living food, it also facilitates the elimination of toxins.

Special Equipment

BLENDER

Although you could probably use any good-quality blender, here are a few recommendations that will make the job even easier.

Total Blender
www.blendtec.com
800-253-6383

This machine has more than enough power to make green smoothies, thoroughly blend raw fruits and vegetables, and make ice cream easily and effortlessly. Its three-peak horsepower motor and patented jar design make fast work of most recipes, and the user-friendly touchpad controls make it simple to operate and easy to clean.

Vita-Mix 5000
www.vitamix.com
800-848-2649

This workhorse is a must-have for any raw vegan kitchen. The Vita-Mix can be used for most tasks and has a large container, so it is convenient if you make large meals.

CERAMIC KNIVES

You will need a durable knife that will cut efficiently, withstand constant washing and storage, and be able to remain sharp without a lot of maintenance. For these and the following reasons, I recommend ceramic knives. .The smooth, polished surface of ceramic knives resists germs and is impervi-

ous to acids, oils, and salts—a boon to the raw foods connoisseur.

When using ceramic knives, care must be taken while cutting items such as fibrous vegetables. You will need a regular, strong (meat) cleaver for opening coconuts. Never use a ceramic knife to do this, nor use one for prying anything open. Due to their extreme hardness, which is why they do not need to be sharpened as often as a steel blade, ceramic knives are brittle. Therefore, a blade may break or chip if adequate care is not taken. The following are two companies that have a reputation for the best ceramic knives.

Boker USA, Inc.
www.bokerusa.com
800-992-6537

Kyocera Advanced Ceramics
www.kyoceraadvancedceramics.com
800-537-0294

CERAMIC PEELER

This is used exactly like a non-ceramic peeler for peeling fruit and vegetables when necessary. However, the cutting edge is ceramic, so like ceramic knives, it won't interact with the flavors of the food you're cutting. The ceramic edge also stays sharp much longer than a metal edge.

DEHYDRATOR AND TEFLEX SHEETS

A food dehydrator is an electrical appliance that removes water (moisture) from food, making it possible to dry fresh foods at home. Properly designed dehydrators work by horizontally blowing gently heated air over their trays, thus evaporating the moisture from the foods placed on the trays. Dehydrated food is very convenient when you are traveling or have a large crop of produce on hand and wish to store it. You can reconstitute anything you have dehydrated simply by adding water to it or soaking it in water.

Teflex sheets are placed on top of dehydrator trays to prevent spillage. They are available coated with high-grade silicone or Teflon. There are also disposable sheets for one-time use made from parchment paper, which are great for easy clean-up.

Here is a source for a good dehydrator and Teflex sheets:

Excalibur Dehydrators and Teflex Sheets
www.excaliburdehydrator.com
1-800-875-4254

Food Processor

A food processor is a versatile kitchen appliance that allows you to chop, slice, shred, grind, and purée almost any food more quickly than is possible by hand. Food processors are available in different sizes and shapes. For the raw vegan kitchen, a European model with double blades is the most effective and efficient.

Grater

Japanese graters typically have finely spaced teeth and are relatively small, light, and easy to care for. They typically are used to grate ginger, wasabi, and daikon radishes, and can be used for garlic as well.

Juicer

The juicers that will best serve your needs for the recipes in this book are single-cutter and twin-gear masticating juicers. Each has advantages and disadvantages, depending on what you are making.

Masticating juicers "chew" (thus the name masticating) the fruit or vegetable to break down the fibers and cell wall structure of the pulp. The next stage is to extract the juice from the broken down pulp by pressing it into a smaller space; thus the pulp is squeezed to discharge the juice. Because these machines operate at slower speeds compared to centrifugal juicers, they produce juice that has less air trapped in it. This means that the juice can be kept slightly longer before oxidation takes place. The single-cutter masticating juicer lends itself very well to making raw vegan ice cream.

With the twin-gear masticating juicer, produce is crushed and pressed between the gears and the juice is pressed out and passed through a screen. There are special cutting points on each of the gears that allow them to handle a wider variety of produce without jamming or clogging. Because you can adjust the amount of pressure without having to stop juicing, you can use a wide variety of produce in one juicing session (such as wheatgrass, other green leafy vegetables, and apples). The juicing process is often slower than with the single-cutter masticating juicer or a centrifugal juicer.

MANDOLINE

A mandoline will help you to cut fruit and vegetables into thin slices, all with an even thickness. It's easy to adjust the thickness of the cut, and you can get julienne cuts simply by switching the blades.

MORTAR AND PESTLE

The primary purpose of using a mortar and pestle in a raw food kitchen is to grind solids into fine powders, but the conditions are highly controlled, so no heat is produced. Because of its ability to effectively manage the grinding and to virtually eliminate contamination from the mortar and pestle set itself, agate is the preferred material to prepare delicate sauces and pastes and for grinding dried spices and herbs.

NUT MILK BAGS

Nut milk bags are nylon mesh bags with a drawstring and a tapered shape for squeezing the liquid from blended fruits, vegetables, nuts, or seeds to make juices and milks.

MILL

Ceramic mills are best for grinding sesame seeds, coarse sea salt, and flaxseeds, and for oats and other grains. The Wolfgang and the Hawo brands stand out.

The main difference between the two mills is the way the grind setting is adjusted. With the Wolfgang mill, the grind setting is adjusted by rotating the hopper, which adjusts the distance between the two grindstones. This means that the Wolfgang mill is infinitely adjustable, from very coarse to very fine. The Hawo mill is adjusted by using a lever that sets the grind. By moving the lever, you adjust the distance between the two stones. This makes it easier to gauge how fine or coarse the setting is because you are able to see different settings from one through ten.

SPIRAL SLICER

These fun tools create spiral strands, ribbons, and slices, so you can make visually appealing shapes and "noodles." The two brands I recommend are Saladacco and Spirooli.

SURIBACHI

A suribachi is a special serrated, glazed clay bowl used with a pestle called a surikogi. It is used in Japanese cuisine for grinding and puréeing nuts, spices, and other foods.

VEGETABLE BRUSH

Japanese natural vegetable brushes are made from coconut fiber and are used for cleaning fresh produce. They are indispensable in a vegan, raw food kitchen. These Japanese "turtle" vegetable brushes are known in Japan as tawashi. Each scrub brush is made from palm fibers that are tightly bound with thick wire. They are the perfect utensil for scrubbing root vegetables and other items without bruising the skins. Tawashi brushes also are handy for getting the crevices of suribachi bowls and sushi mats clean, and are convenient for scrubbing wooden cutting boards and bamboo utensils. They are inexpensive and will outlast regular synthetic brushes.

Resources

SERENITY SPACES RESOURCE GUIDE

The Raw Bakery
Raw grains, including truly raw oat groats and germinated brown rice. Also, ceramic knives.
Phone: (310) 854-2078
E-mail: dorit@serenityspaces.org
Web site: www.serenityspaces.org

Raw Lifestyle Film Festival
Organized and created by Dorit, this is an international event celebrating and unifying the raw and conscious living communities through films.
Phone: (310) 854-2078
Email: rawfilmfest@serenityspaces.org
Web site: www.serenityspaces.org

Serenity Spaces Community
Raw lifestyle support and group membership.
Phone: (310) 854-2078
E-mail: serenityspaces@yahoogroups.com
Web site: www.rawlifestylesupportgroup.com
Web site: www.serenityspaces.org

ADDITIONAL RESOURCES

American BlueGreen
Himalayan Crystal Salt.
Phone: (877) 224-4872
Web site: americanbluegreen.com

The Chopra Centre at La Costa Resort and Spa
Panchakarma, meditation, Ayurvedic treatments.
Phone: (888) 424-6772, ext. 1111
E-mail: info@chopra.com
Web site: www.chopra.com

GeneFit Nutrition
The exclusive U.S. importer of fresh durian, untreated young Thai coconuts, and palm nectar.
Phone: (866) EAT PURE or (310) 310-237-6456
Web site: www.genefitnutrition.com
E-mail: info@genefitnutrition.com

Gold Mine Natural Foods
Nama Shoyu, raw food supplies, raw sauerkraut, raw cultured vegetables, umeboshi, dried mushrooms, Flower of the Ocean sea minerals, Celtic sea salt, sea vegetables, raw nuts, mesquite meal, rapadura, raw carob powder, more.
Phone: (800) 475-3663
E-mail: customerservice@goldminenatural-foods.com
Web: www.goldminenaturalfoods.com

The Grain & Salt Society
Celtic sea salt and Flower of the Ocean sea minerals.
Phone: (800) 867-7258
E-mail: info@celtic-seasalt.com
Web site: www.celticseasalt.com

Living Tree Community Foods
Raw coconut butter, wild rice, mesquite powder, nut butters, maca, agave nectar, living oils, sun-dried olives, and more.
Phone: (800) 260-5534 or (510) 526-7106
E-mail: info@livingtreecommunity.com
Web site: www.livingtreecommunity.com

Madhava
Raw organic agave nectar.
Phone: (303) 823-5166
E-mail: info@madhavahoney.com
Web site: www.madhavahoney.com

The Noah Center
Outstanding workshops on health and healing.
Phone: (413) 528-0297
E-mail: info@noahcenter.org
Web site: www.noahcenter.org

Rejuvenative Foods
Raw nut and seed butters, cultured vegetables.
Phone: (800) 805-7957
E-mail: mail@rejuvenative.com
Web site: www.rejuvenative.com

Ruth's Hemp Foods
Sprouted flax, maca, and hemp powders.
Phone: (416) 588-4209
E-mail: info@ruthshempfoods.com
Web site: www.ruthshempfoods.com

Sproutman
Classes in the U.S. and books on sprouting by Steve Meyerowitz, Sproutman.
Phone: (413) 528-5200
Web site: www.Sproutman.com
E-mail: info@Sproutman.com

Sustainable Events Group
Specializes in green, sustainable, eco-friendly event planning and execution around the world. The catering menu is mainly organic raw vegan and living foods, but a menu of some cooked organic vegan food is also available to accommodate everyone.
Phone: (310) 854-2078
E-mail: serenityspaces@yahoo.com
Web site: www.serenityspaces.org

Toronto Sprouts
Fresh sprouts and sprouting classes and other events with Dorit in Canada.
Phone: (416) 535-3111
E-mail: info@torontosprouts.com
Web site: www.torontosprouts.com

Tribest
Juice extractors, personal blenders, sprouting supplies, water distillers, ceramic knives, and grain mills.
Phone: (888) 254-7336
E-mail: service@greenpower.com
Web site: www.tribest.com

VISION
E3Live and E3AFA.
Phone: (888) 800-7070
E-mail: sales@e3live.com
Web site: www.e3live.com

Guidelines for Raw Nuts and Seeds

Here are a few tips for purchasing, storing, and using raw nuts and seeds:
- Purchase only organic nuts and seeds.
- Most cashews that are labeled raw are not truly raw. The only truly raw cashews currently available in the United States are imported from Indonesia and Bolivia.
- Rinse nuts and seeds well. Then soak them in purified or distilled water to cover.
- If nuts and seeds are not being used immediately after they have been soaked, rinse them and then dehydrate them.
- Store all raw nuts and seeds in the refrigerator.

Soaking Nuts, Seeds, and Grains

Most nuts can be soaked for eight to twelve hours; they should be rinsed before using. If you soak them longer than this, discard the soak water and rinse them every eight hours. For sprouting information, please consult a book dedicated to sprouting, or study with a reputable teacher who specializes in sprouting. Nuts that will not sprout include cashews, walnuts, pecans, and Brazil nuts; these should just be soaked, rinsed, and eaten or dehydrated.

Suggested Soaking Times for Germination

Nut, Seed, Grain	Soaking Time	Nut, Seed, Grain	Soaking Time
Almonds	8 to 12 hours	Pine nuts	20 minutes to 4 hours
Amaranth	3 to 6 hours	Pumpkin seeds	6 to 8 hours
Barley	6 to 8 hours	Quinoa	3 to 4 hours
Buckwheat	6 hours only	Sesame seeds, hulled	8 hours
Chickpeas	12 to 48 hours	Sesame seeds, unhulled	4 to 6 hours
Flaxseeds	12 to 48 hours	Spelt	6 to 7 hours
Kamut	7 hours	Sunflower seeds, hulled*	4 to 8 hours
Mustard seeds	5 to 8 hours	Teff	3 to 4 hours
Oats	8 to 24 hours	Walnuts	24 to 48 hours
Pecans	24 to 68 hours		

*Sunflower seeds become bitter if soaked for more than a few hours.

Breakfast Options

Since the word breakfast means "to break a fast," which hopefully took place overnight, it follows that we ought to first rehydrate ourselves in the morning. This, of course, is best done with clean, pure water. For additional hydration, you'll find many choices in the Beverage chapter (pages 22–32) and Liquid Meals chapter (pages 196–219) to continue the process. If you feel the need to consume more nourishment, this chapter provides many options.

Should you choose to use the recipes that call for oats, please make sure that they are truly raw. Most oats are heat-treated with steam or infrared light in order to extend their shelf life. You will know if they are raw because only raw oats can be germinated. To do this, it is best to soak the raw oats for three to twelve hours before using.

In addition to oats for your morning breakfast, any green drinks are worthy choices to start the day. In fact, if your time tends to be largely spent in meetings or taking care of someone, I strongly suggest that you fortify yourself with green drinks before starting the day's activities. If you are pressed for time, there is always E3Live (see page 43) to use as a cornerstone to starting your day with greens.

Apple Crisp ....

10 apples, peeled and sliced

1 lemon, juiced

½ teaspoon ground cinnamon

½ cup raw walnuts, finely chopped

½ cup raw almonds, ground

½ cup raw oat groats, ground and soaked

½ cup agave nectar

⅛ teaspoon Celtic sea salt

½ cup raw grapeseed oil or walnut oil

Combine the apples, lemon juice, and ¼ teaspoon of the cinnamon, and transfer to a glass baking dish. Combine the walnuts, almonds, oats, agave nectar, remaining ¼ teaspoon cinnamon, and salt. Drizzle in the oil and mix well, using clean hands, until the mixture resembles course crumbs. Spread the mixture evenly over the apples, and place in a dehydrator at 105 to 108 degrees F until the topping is brown. Remove from the dehydrator and serve.

Apricot Carrot Bread .... YIELD: 2 TO 4 SERVINGS

1 cup sprouted flaxseeds, ground

6 to 8 dried apricots, soaked for 4 to 6 hours

2 to 3 carrots, finely grated

2 teaspoons agave nectar

½ teaspoon ground cinnamon

½ teaspoon almond extract

Dash of Celtic sea salt

⅓ cup raisins

Put the ground flaxseeds in a mixing bowl. Drain the soaked apricots, and put them in a food processor fitted with the S blade. Add the grated carrots, agave nectar, cinnamon, almond extract, and salt. Pulse until everything blends into a ball. Taste for sweetness, and add more agave nectar if needed.

Transfer the mixture to the bowl with the ground flaxseeds, and add the raisins. Mix well. Pack into a loaf pan, and put in a dehydrator at 106 to 108 degrees F for 5 to 6 hours. Remove from the loaf pan, turn the bread over on the dehydrating tray, and return it to the dehydrator until it is completely dry on the inside.

NOTE: This may be formed into individual portions rather than a single loaf, if preferred.

Buckwheat Crackers .... <small>YIELD: 6 TO 8 SERVINGS</small>

Use these crackers as toast or as you would use any bread for breakfast. This can also be used for pizza crust. Just make the crackers thicker so they can hold up to moist toppings.

8 cups water

4 cups raw buckwheat groats

½ medium, sweet onion (optional)

½ cup nutritional yeast (optional)

½ cup fresh basil

½ to 1 tablespoon cayenne (optional)

1 to 2 tablespoons ground sprouted flaxseeds

½ teaspoon fresh or dried oregano

Combine the water and buckwheat groats in a large bowl, and let soak for 8 to 12 hours or overnight. The groats will get very gooey. Drain and rinse the buckwheat until the water runs clear. Sprout the buckwheat for 2 to 3 days.

Combine the sprouted buckwheat and the remaining ingredients in a high-powered blender or food processor fitted with the S blade, and process until the desired consistency is achieved. If necessary, add water sparingly to facilitate processing.

Spread the mixture onto waxed paper or parchment paper to a thickness of ¼ to ½ inch. Make slash marks every 2 to 3 inches for better drying. Dehydrate at 107 to 120 degrees F. After 4 to 6 hours, flip the crackers over and peel off the paper. Continue to dehydrate until they reach the desired crispness.

NOTES: An equal amount of slippery elm powder or ground psyllium husks can be used sparingly in place of the flaxseeds, if preferred.

• For a more intense and immediate flavor, sprinkle more spices on top of the crackers while they are still wet.

Whole Grain Cereal ....

3 tablespoons rye berries, raw oat groats, or a combination of both, ground

½ cup ground or chopped raw nuts

½ cup seasonal fresh fruit (optional)

1 teaspoon agave nectar

Dash of freshly squeezed lemon juice

1 apple

2 cups Cashew Milk (page 40) or Almond Milk (page 34)

Add enough water to the ground grain to moisten it, and let soak for 5 to 12 hours. Add the nuts, fresh fruit, agave nectar, and lemon juice. Grate the apple and immediately add it to the cereal before the apple turns brown. (To prevent browning, use a ceramic grater.) Portion into cereal bowls. Serve with the Cashew Milk.

NOTE: Replace the fresh fruit with dried fruit, if preferred.

Hearty Seed Porridge .... YIELD: 2 SERVINGS

If you like, serve this porridge with any of the nut milk recipes found in this book.

½ cup raw almonds. soaked

½ cup flaxseeds, soaked

½ cup raw sunflower seeds, sprouted

2 to 3 celery stalks, chopped

2 to 3 tablespoons Vitamineral Green (see page 15)

1 tablespoon spirulina powder

1½ teaspoons stevia powder

Combine all the ingredients in a high-powered blender or food processor fitted with the S blade, and process into a smooth, creamy purée. If necessary, blend in batches and add water sparingly to facilitate processing.

Mixed Fruit and Nut Granola..........

YIELD: 2 TO 3 SERVINGS

½ cup raw hazelnuts, soaked and dehydrated

1 tablespoon dried Incan berries

1 tablespoon dried mulberries

1 tablespoon raw pine nuts

1 tablespoon unsweetened shredded dried coconut

1 tablespoon yacon syrup or agave nectar

½ teaspoon ground cinnamon

½ teaspoon ground cardamom (optional)

1 cup Almond Milk (page 34) or Macadamia Nut Milk (page 34)

1 banana

Combine the hazelnuts, Incan berries, mulberries, pine nuts, coconut, yacon syrup, cinnamon, and optional cardamom in a bowl. Add the nut milk and stir. Thinly slice the banana directly into the bowl, and mix well. Add more spices and/or sweetener to suit your taste.

Mucus Mover ....

YIELD: 2 CUPS

This juice makes a great breakfast when you are experiencing a cold or flu symptoms.

2 carrots

2 celery stalks

1 radish

Push the carrots, celery, and radish through the hopper of a juicer. If the taste of the radish is too strong, add another carrot or an apple.

Pecan Porridge .... YIELD: 4 TO 6 SERVINGS

This makes a hearty, filling, and extremely delicious breakfast for winter mornings.

2 cups firm young Thai coconut flesh

1¼ cups young Thai coconut water

1 cup raw almonds

1 cup raw pecans

3 or 4 pitted dates (optional)

1 teaspoon raw coconut oil

½ teaspoon vanilla extract

½ teaspoon Celtic sea salt

Dash of ground cinnamon

Dash of ground nutmeg

Place all the ingredients in a high-powered blender, and pulse 3 or 4 times, just until well combined but still chunky. For a softer, smoother consistency, pulse a few more times.

Quinoa Cereal .... YIELD: 2 TO 3 SERVINGS

1 cup quinoa, soaked and sprouted

½ cup Almond Milk (page 34) or Cashew Milk (page 40)

2 or 3 pitted dates, finely chopped

1 banana

1 tablespoon agave nectar or yacon syrup

¼ teaspoon vanilla extract, or a snippet of fresh vanilla bean

Dash of Celtic sea salt

Place all the ingredients in a high-powered blender, and pulse until evenly combined.

Quinoa Fruit Salad .... YIELD: 4 TO 5 SERVINGS

1 cup quinoa, soaked and sprouted

¼ cup Cashew Milk (page 40) or Almond Milk (page 34)

3 to 5 pitted dates, finely chopped

1½ cups sliced strawberries

1 cup sliced mandarin oranges

2 kiwis, peeled and sliced

⅓ cup chopped fresh mint

2 tablespoons freshly squeezed orange juice

Place the quinoa sprouts in a large bowl. Combine the Cashew Milk and dates in a high-powered blender, and process until smooth. Pour over the quinoa sprouts. Add the remaining ingredients and mix well.

VARIATION—WARM WINTER FRUIT SALAD: After combining the quinoa sprouts and blended milk, place the bowl in a dehydrator and dehydrate the sprouts at 108 degrees F for 1 hour. Add the fruits and orange juice just before serving. Garnish with the mint.

Quick Breakfast .... YIELD: 1 TO 2 SERVINGS

1 medium pear, cored and diced

½ cup Cashew Milk (page 40)

2 to 3 tablespoons Raw Granola (page 29)

Put the diced pear into a cereal bowl. Add the milk. Put the granola in the bowl, and mix well before serving.

Raw Granola..........................

6 cups raw oat groats

1 teaspoon ground cinnamon

2 cups unsweetened shredded dried coconut

½ cup raisins

2 tablespoons Raw Almond Butter (page 160)

1 teaspoon vanilla extract

1 cup raw sunflower seeds, sprouted

2 cups raw almonds or pecans

Agave nectar

Coarsely grind the oats in a food processor fitted with the S blade, or in a grain mill or coffee grinder, gradually adding the cinnamon. Transfer to a mixing bowl.

Place the coconut, raisins, almond butter, and vanilla extract in a food processor. Pulse until combined. Add the sunflower sprouts and pulse. Add the oats to this mixture, and pulse until they are evenly mixed in. Add the almonds and pulse a few times, just until they are coarsely chopped (the mixture should be crunchy). Sweeten with agave nectar to taste, and mix well.

Spread the mixture on a dehydrator tray, and dehydrate at 105 degrees F for 4 to 6 hours, turning from time to time. Continue to dehydrate until the mixture is totally dry and crispy.

Sweet Potato Pudding .... YIELD: 2 SERVINGS

1 sweet potato or yam

1 cup coconut flesh

2 tablespoons yacon syrup or agave nectar (optional)

1 teaspoon raw coconut oil

Dash of ground nutmeg

Dash of Allspice (page 169)

Dash of Himalayan salt

Cut the yam or sweet potato into small chunks. Transfer to a food processor fitted with the S blade, and add the remaining ingredients. Alternatively, place in a high-powered blender and add the remaining ingredients along with a small amount of coconut water. Use a plunger to keep the mixture moving.

Process until the mixture is the consistency of pudding. Add more yacon syrup or spices to suit your taste. Let stand for about 1 hour before serving.

Breakfast on the Road .... YIELD: 10 TO 12 SERVINGS

This recipe is great to take when you are traveling.

1 cup dried apricots, finely chopped

1 cup other dried fruit, finely chopped

1 cup raw almonds, ground

1 cup raw walnuts, chopped

Fruit juice, as needed

Combine the fruits and nuts in a medium bowl. Form into bite-size balls. If the mixture is too dry to hold together, add a small amount of fruit juice.

Breakfast Parfait .... YIELD: 4 SERVINGS

1 ⅓ cups Applesauce (page 176)

1 cup (about 6 ounces) pitted prunes

1 ½ cups ground raw oats, soaked overnight

1 cup Sesame Milk (page 53)

4 whole pitted prunes, for garnish

1 teaspoon ground cinnamon

Have ready four 9- or 10-ounce stemmed goblets. Combine the applesauce and 1 cup prunes in a high-powered blender, and process until smooth. For each goblet, layer ¼ cup of the soaked oats, ½ cup of the applesauce and prune mixture, and 1 to 2 tablespoons of the Sesame Milk. Repeat the layers and top with 2 tablespoons of the oats and additional Sesame Milk to cover. Garnish with a whole prune and a dash of cinnamon. Serve immediately, or refrigerate for up to 4 hours before serving.

Orange Compote with Oats ...... YIELD: 6 SERVINGS

Serve this compote topped with Date Butter (page 152), or drain it and place it on lettuce leaves.

2 naval oranges, peeled and separated into segments

1 apple or pear, diced

½ cup seedless red or green grapes, cut in half

1 banana, thinly sliced

2 tablespoons freshly squeezed orange juice

½ cup ground raw oats, soaked for 8 to 12 hours

Cut the orange segments in half. Toss together the oranges, apple, grapes, banana, and orange juice in a medium bowl. Sprinkle the oats over the fruit and toss lightly. Serve immediately.

Apple Oatmeal ....

½ cup (about ½ medium) diced Golden Delicious apple

⅓ cup apple juice

1 cup Macadamia Nut Milk (page 34)

⅛ teaspoon Celtic sea salt (optional)

Dash of ground cinnamon

Dash of ground nutmeg

⅓ cup ground raw oats, soaked overnight

Combine the apples, apple juice, nut milk, salt, cinnamon, and nutmeg in a small bowl. Stir in the ground oats. Cover and let stand 10 to 15 minutes before serving.

Apricot Jam with Strawberries

Yield: 4 servings

⅓ cup chopped apricot flesh

3 tablespoon Cashew Milk (page 40), Almond Milk (page 34),
   or Macadamia Nut Milk

1 teaspoon ground cinnamon

2 pints strawberries, stemmed and diced

Combine the apricots, nut milk, and cinnamon in a high-powered blender, and pulse until combined. Transfer to a small bowl and add the strawberries. Toss gently to combine, and serve.

*B*everages

Doesn't a glass of freshly squeezed vegetable or fruit juice sound delightful? How about a glass of coconut water that tastes like nectar of the gods? If you want something for the "cocktail hour," choose a glass of untreated palm nectar, which I call "raw champagne straight from the heavens."

Almond Milk .... YIELD: ABOUT 5 CUPS

This is an essential recipe for novices as well as anyone who is lactose intolerant but enjoys the flavor of dairy-based dishes.

2 cups raw almonds, soaked 8 to 12 hours

3 to 4 cups water

Combine ½ cup of the almonds and about 1 cup or more of the water in a high-powered blender, and process on high for 2 to 3 minutes, or until the mixture is completely smooth and creamy. Place a nut milk bag or a cheesecloth bag over a wide-mouth container and pour the milk through it. Squeeze to remove all the liquid. Put the pulp in the freezer to use in other recipes. Process the remaining almonds and water in batches in the same fashion. Serve immediately or thoroughly chilled.

NOTE: For a sweet-flavored version of this milk, see More Nut Milk, page 48.

Macadamia Nut Milk .... YIELD: 4 TO 5 SERVINGS

This nutritious milk is delicious as a beverage, or it can be used to complement the cereals in the Breakfast Options chapter.

2 to 3 cups water

1 cup raw macadamia nuts

¼ cup raw pine nuts

1 vanilla bean, scraped

1 cardamom seed

Dash of ground nutmeg

Combine all the ingredients in a high-powered blender, and process on high until completely smooth and creamy. Serve immediately or thoroughly chilled.

Hemp Milk .... YIELD: 3 TO 4 CUPS

This is highly recommended for vegan athletes.

1 cup raw hempseeds

3 tablespoons raw almonds

2 cups water

1 banana

1 tablespoon yacon syrup or agave nectar

1 tablespoon raw hemp oil (optional)

Dash of Allspice (page 169)

Soak the hempseeds and almonds in water to cover for 24 hours. Be sure to change the water about every 8 hours. Drain, rinse, and place in a high-powered blender with the 2 cups water, banana, yacon syrup, optional hemp oil, and Allspice. Process until smooth, then strain through a nut milk bag or cheesecloth.

NOTE: This milk is best consumed immediately, although it will keep for about 48 hours in a sealed container in the refrigerator.

Coconut Milk .... YIELD: ABOUT 1 CUP

Use this for any occasion when milk is desired, or add it to ice cream and smoothies.

1 coconut, water and flesh

Put the coconut flesh through the hopper of a heavy-duty masticating juicer. If necessary, add a very small amount of the coconut water. Refrigerate immediately.

Apple Juice Supreme .... Yield: 2 cups

    1 pint strawberries, stems removed
    1 cup apple juice
    1 pear

Combine all the ingredients in a high-powered blender, and process until smooth. Serve thoroughly chilled.

Apple Cider Vinegar Drink ...... Yield: 1 serving

This drink can be taken up to three times a day. Sip it slowly rather than gulping it down.

    6 to 8 ounces water
    1 to 2 teaspoons raw apple cider vinegar

Combine the water and vinegar in a serving cup or glass. Stir well and serve.

Banana Manna .... Yield: 2 servings

To boost the calcium content, use raw black sesame tahini.

    2 frozen bananas
    2/3 cup water
    2 tablespoons raw tahini
    1 tablespoon raw honey or agave nectar
    1 teaspoon vanilla extract
    Dash of ground cinnamon

Combine all the ingredients in a high-powered blender, and process until creamy.

Banana Berry Smoothie .... YIELD: 4 TO 5 CUPS

2 cups water

1 cup sliced frozen bananas

1 cup freshly squeezed orange juice

¼ cup fresh or frozen mixed berries

3 to 5 pitted dates (optional)

3 tablespoons raw cashews

Fresh mint (optional)

Combine all the ingredients in a high-powered blender, and process until completely smooth and creamy. Serve thoroughly chilled.

Banana Cherry Milk Shake

YIELD: 3 TO 4 CUPS

2 to 3 cups Almond Milk (page 34)

1 frozen, very ripe banana

1 cup pitted cherries

6 to 8 pitted honey dates

Combine all the ingredients in a high-powered blender, and process until the desired texture is achieved.

NOTE: For a thicker shake, use only 2 cups Almond Milk.

Maca Supreme Smoothie ....

This makes a very nourishing breakfast drink.

1 cup Sesame Milk (page 53)

1 frozen banana

1 tablespoon maca powder

1 teaspoon mesquite powder

Combine all the ingredients in a high-powered blender, and process until smooth. Serve at once or thoroughly chilled.

Hemp Smoothie .... Yield : 1 serving

1 cup Almond Milk (page 34)

1 frozen banana

2 to 3 pitted dates

1 tablespoon hemp powder

Combine all the ingredients in a high-powered blender, and process until smooth. Serve at once or thoroughly chilled.

Banana Milk Shake .... Yield: 2½ cups

2 cups Almond Milk (page 34) or
Cashew Milk (page 40)

1 to 2 frozen bananas

4 to 6 pitted dates

2 to 4 ice cubes (optional)

Dash of ground cinnamon

Dash of ground nutmeg

Combine all the ingredients in a high-powered blender, and process until completely smooth and creamy. Serve thoroughly chilled.

Beet Juice ....

To get the full benefits, drink this juice slowly and mindfully.

4 apples

½ beet

1 slice fresh ginger

Push all the ingredients through the hopper of a juicer. Pour the juice into a wine glass and serve.

Insomniac's Blueberry Nightcap

YIELD: ABOUT 1½ CUPS

1 cup water

½ cup fresh blueberries, or ¼ to ½ cup frozen blueberries

2 tablespoons E3Live

1 to 2 tablespoons agave nectar

1 teaspoon raw black sesame tahini

Dash of Celtic sea salt

Combine all the ingredients in a high-powered blender and process on low to medium speed for 30 to 45 seconds. Chew every morsel you place in your mouth mindfully, calmly, and slowly at least 30 minutes before retiring to bed.

Cabbage Carrot Juice .... YIELD: 2 CUPS

¼ head cabbage

1 slice fresh ginger

2 to 3 carrots

1 apple

Wrap the ginger in a cabbage leaf. Push the cabbage through the hopper of a juicer with the carrots and apple. Drink immediately.

Carrot Parsley Drink .... YIELD: 1 TO 2 CUPS

1 handful fresh parsley

4 to 6 carrots

1 parsley sprig, for garnish

Bunch up the parsley and push it through hopper of a juicer along with the carrots. Pour into a long-stemmed glass. Garnish with the parsley sprig and serve.

Cashew Milk .... YIELD: 5 TO 6 CUPS

3 to 4 cups water

2 cups raw cashews

Combine the water and cashews in a high-powered blender, and process until completely smooth and creamy. Serve immediately or thoroughly chilled.

NOTE: For a creamier, thicker milk, use less water.

Cherry Smoothie .... YIELD: 3 TO 4 CUPS

2 cups pitted cherries

1 cup Cashew Milk (page 40)

½ cup ice (optional)

5 or 6 pitted medjool dates

Combine all the ingredients in a high-powered blender, and process until completely smooth and creamy. Serve immediately or thoroughly chilled.

Chilled Tea .... YIELD: 1 QUART

This is the raw version of iced tea.

1 quart water, more or less as needed

1 orange, peeled and separated into segments

1 Granny Smith apple, sliced

½ cup ice (optional)

1 spearmint sprig

1 tablespoon stevia powder or liquid or agave nectar

2 lime wedges

Combine the water, orange, apple, ice, and spearmint in a high-powered blender, and process until smooth. Sweeten with stevia to taste. Serve immediately or thoroughly chilled. To serve, pour into a chilled glass, and place a wedge of lime on the side of the glass.

Cleansing Juice .... YIELD: ABOUT 2 CUPS

3 to 4 carrots

1 apple, quartered

½ to 1 beet, quartered

1 (thumb-size) piece fresh ginger

¼ small lemon

Use the carrots to push the apple, beet, ginger, and lemon (in that order) through the hopper of a juicer. Drink immediately.

Digestive Calmer ....

Drink this calming beverage slowly and mindfully.

1 to 2 Granny Smith apples, chopped

⅓ cup spinach juice

¼ cup cabbage juice

¼ cup cucumber juice

¼ cup celery juice

2 tablespoons green pepper juice

Combine all the ingredients in a high-powered blender, and process until smooth.

Digestive Kuzu Cream .... YIELD: 1 SERVING

This recipe makes a thick cream that is almost like a pudding. If you prefer a thinner drink, reduce the amount of kuzu to one rounded teaspoon.

1 cup warm water

1½ teaspoons kuzu

1 pitted umeboshi plum, minced, or 1 teaspoon umeboshi paste

½ to 1 teaspoon Nama Shoyu (optional)

¼ to ½ teaspoon ginger juice (see note)

Dissolve the kuzu starch in the water, and stir with a spoon. Add the umeboshi plum and mix well until it dissolves. Stir constantly until the kuzu thickens and becomes translucent. Place it in the sun or in a dehydrator, if necessary. Add the optional Nama Shoyu and ginger juice to taste.

NOTE: To make ginger juice, finely grate fresh ginger and squeeze it with your hands to extract the juice.

Ume-Kuzu Digestive Drink ....

1 pitted umeboshi plum

1 tablespoon kuzu

1 cup warm water

1 drop Nama Shoyu

Break the umeboshi plum into small pieces. Add the kuzu and 1 tablespoon of the water. Mix until the kuzu blends into a paste, taking care that there are no lumps. Add the remainder of the water, and place in the sun or in a dehydrator at 118 degrees F for about 30 minutes, stirring frequently. Stir in the Nama Shoyu.

NOTES: If the kuzu dissolves easily, the drink can be served immediately without placing it in the sun or a dehydrator.

• Be sure to use only kuzu; do not substitute arrowroot.

E3Live Smoothie...........................

This is the perfect choice for an energizing and nutritious breakfast.

1 cup Almond Milk (page 34)

2 bananas

½ cup non-citrus frozen fruit (optional)

1 to 2 tablespoon E3Live, or 2 to 6 capsules E3AFA, or 1 to 3 teaspoons
    E3AFA crystal flakes

¼ teaspoon vanilla extract

Combine all the ingredients in a high-powered blender, and process until smooth. Serve immediately.

Ginger Champagne .... YIELD: 2 TO 3 SERVINGS

You and your guests will be delighted with this nutritious drink if you serve it at parties.

1 slice (¼ inch thick) fresh ginger
1 apple, quartered

½ cup palm nectar, chilled

Push the ginger through the hopper of a juicer with the apple. Pour a small amount in a champagne flute. Fill rest of the glass with the palm nectar and serve.

Ginger Delight .... YIELD: 2 TO 3 SERVINGS

This makes a great winter beverage.

1 slice (¼ inch thick) fresh ginger
4 to 5 carrots

1 apple, quartered

Push the ginger through the hopper of a juicer while alternating between the carrots and apple pieces. If you prefer to use a high-powered blender, add lots of water and blend on the highest speed until a thin consistency is achieved.

Grape Spritzer .... YIELD: 2 TO 3 SERVINGS

Here is another version of a raw, nonalcoholic champagne that will astonish your guests.

1 to 2 bunches grapes

1 cup palm nectar

Process the grapes in a high-powered blender until smooth. Add a little water, if necessary. Squeeze through a nut milk bag. Fill chilled glasses with half of the grape juice and half of the palm nectar, and serve immediately.

Holiday Beverage ....

This is a great substitute for eggnog or other alcoholic beverages at family gatherings and parties.

4 cups apple juice

2 frozen bananas

1 cup freshly squeezed orange juice

1 vanilla bean, scraped

½ teaspoon ground cinnamon

¼ teaspoon ground nutmeg

Dash of ground cardamom

Combine all the ingredients in a high-powered blender, and process until smooth.

Juice Delight .... YIELD: 1 TO 2 SERVINGS

This is a quick pick-me-up and a children's favorite.

3 carrots

1 apple, quartered

Put the carrots and apple though the hopper of a juicer. Drink immediately.

Lemonade .... YIELD: 1 SERVING

This is a simple version of fresh lemonade.

1 cup water

½ lemon, juiced

1 teaspoon rapadura, yacon syrup, or
  agave nectar

1 spearmint sprig

Ice (optional)

Combine all the ingredients in a high-powered blender and process on low. Add more sweetener to taste, if desired. Serve chilled.

Liver Flush Cocktail .... YIELD: 1 SERVING

Drink this first thing in the morning.

1 cup freshly squeezed grapefruit or orange juice

1 tablespoon raw olive oil

½ to 1 tablespoons chopped fresh ginger

1 to 2 garlic cloves

Combine all the ingredients in a high-powered blender, and process until smooth.

NOTE: After consuming this beverage, wait one hour before eating. Continue this morning ritual for ten days. Skip a week and then repeat the entire routine.

Mango Nectar .... YIELD: 2 TO 3 SERVINGS

This is really beneficial when you are feeling low on energy.

2 to 3 mangoes

½ papaya

1 cup coconut water

Cut the peeled mango and papaya flesh into chunks, and place in a high-powered blender. Add the coconut water, and process until completely smooth. Serve thoroughly chilled.

Melon Magic .... YIELD: 1 TO 2 SERVINGS

This makes for a great thirst quencher on a hot summer's day.

1 small honeydew melon

¼ lime or lemon

Wash the skin of the melon thoroughly with a vegetable brush. Remove the seeds, cut it into pieces, and process it through the hopper of a juicer or in a high-powered blender with a small wedge of lime or lemon. Serve immediately or thoroughly chilled.

46 CELEBRATING OUR RAW NATURE

Midmorning Perk-Up ....

In addition to giving you a midmorning boost, this drink is great to serve at festive functions.

2 to 3 young Thai coconuts

2 to 3 fresh or frozen bananas

3 to 5 fresh figs, washed, stemmed, and quartered

Mint sprigs

Pour the coconut water into a high-powered blender. Scoop out the flesh of the coconuts, and add it to the blender along with the bananas. Process until very smooth. Add the figs, and process again until completely smooth. Pour into champagne or wine glasses, and garnish with mint sprigs.

Mint Lemonade .... YIELD: 2 SERVINGS

2 cups water

½ lemon

1 to 2 tablespoons agave nectar

1 mint sprig

Combine all the ingredients in a high-powered blender, and process until smooth. Serve thoroughly chilled.

Minty Apple Drink .... YIELD: 1 TO 2 SERVINGS

1 small handful fresh spearmint

4 apples, quartered

Push the spearmint through the hopper of a juicer with the apples. Serve thoroughly chilled.

More Nut Milk .... YIELD: 2 TO 4 CUPS

This is the sweetened version of cashew or almond milk. It is extremely popular and versatile, and is the perfect replacement for cow's milk or soymilk.

2 to 4 cups Cashew Milk (page 40) or Almond Milk (page 34)

7 to 9 pitted dates, or 2 tablespoons yacon syrup or agave nectar

1 vanilla bean, scraped

¼ teaspoon ground nutmeg

¼ teaspoon ground cinnamon

Combine all the ingredients in a high-powered blender, and process until smooth and creamy.

Morning Glory .... YIELD: 3 TO 4 SERVINGS

This makes a very quick and nutritious breakfast.

1 whole cantaloupe   Mint sprigs (optional)

Wash the skin of the cantaloupe thoroughly with a vegetable brush. Cut the cantaloupe in half, and scoop out and discard the seeds. Cut into pieces and feed through the hopper of a juicer. Pour into wine glasses, and garnish with mint sprigs, if desired. Drink immediately.

Morning Tonic .... YIELD: 1 SERVING

This is a delicious winter beverage.

1 grapefruit, peeled   1 slice fresh ginger

1 Red Delicious apple, quartered

Push the grapefruit and ginger through the hopper of a juicer with the apple. Alternatively, place all the ingredients in a high-powered blender along with a small amount of water, and process on high until smooth.

Morning Sunrise .... Yield: 1 serving

This is a great substitute for coffee.

2 oranges, peeled and quartered   3 carrots

Push the oranges through the hopper of a juicer with the carrots. Pour into a wine glass and serve immediately.

NOTE: I have used this to help many clients release coffee beverages from their morning routines, and they have all claimed success with it.

Morning Mover .... Yield: 1 serving

1 large apple, or 2 small apples, quartered   1 orange, peeled and quartered

2 ripe pears

Use the apple to push the soft pears and the orange through the hopper of a juicer. Alternatively, combine all of the ingredients in a high-powered blender along with a small amount of water, and process until smooth.

NOTES: If you use a high-powered blender for this drink due, you will benefit from the fiber that would otherwise be wasted when the fruit is put through a juicer.

• This drink is known to assist in moving the bowels.

Nectarine Drink .... Yield: 2 servings

4 or 5 pitted nectarines   1 apple, quartered

1 frozen banana   1 cup freshly squeezed orange juice

Combine all the ingredients in a high-powered blender, and process until smooth. Serve in tall glasses.

Papaya Delight ....

This is a quick and delicious way to boost your supply of digestive enzymes.

1 green papaya, peeled, seeded, and sliced

2 cups coconut water

1 Red Delicious apple, quartered

½ teaspoon freshly squeezed lime juice

Combine all the ingredients in a high-powered blender, and process until smooth. Serve in wine glasses or champagne flutes.

Papaya Milk Shake ....

This is a very creamy and rich drink.

2 to 4 cups water

2 cups raw macadamia nuts

½ to 1 papaya, peeled, seeded, and sliced

4 to 5 pitted dates

3 or 4 ice cubes

Combine all the ingredients in a high-powered blender, and process until smooth. Pour into glasses, and top each glass with a little umbrella for decoration. Serve immediately.

Piña Colada ....

2 cups coconut water

½ very ripe papaya, peeled, seeded, and sliced

1 cup pineapple chunks

½ cup ice (optional)

Combine all the ingredients in a high-powered blender, and process until smooth. Pour into chilled glasses, and top each glass with a little umbrella for decoration. Serve immediately.

Pineapple Paradise ....

½ pineapple with skin, chopped

2 cups coconut water

2 Red Delicious or Granny Smith apples, quartered

½ teaspoon freshly squeezed lime juice

Combine all the ingredients in a high-powered blender, and process until smooth. Pour into chilled glasses, and top each glass with a little umbrella for decoration. Serve immediately.

Pineapple Smoothie ....

2 cups chopped pineapple

1 cup apple juice

2 frozen bananas

Combine all the ingredients in a high-powered blender, and process until smooth. Serve immediately.

Pink Lemonade ....

2 cups chilled water

½ cup fresh strawberries, stems removed

½ cup frozen strawberries

½ lemon, juiced

1 teaspoon yacon syrup or agave nectar

Combine the water, fresh and frozen strawberries, and lemon juice in a high-powered blender, and process until smooth. Sweeten with the yacon syrup to taste, and blend briefly on low.

Quick Apple Lemonade ....

Perfect for a hot summer afternoon.

3 to 4 apples   ¼ lemon

Juice the apples and lemon separately. Combine the juices, and serve thoroughly chilled.

Raw Party Champagne ....

This is great for parties!

2 apples   1 lemon wedge

1 large bunch grapes   2 cups chilled water (optional)

Push all the fruits through the hopper of a juicer. If using the chilled water, mix everything together in a pitcher. Chill thoroughly, and serve in champagne flutes.

Raw Ginger Ale ....

This recipe is a favorite with men.

1 bunch green grapes   1 slice fresh ginger

½ apple, sliced   1 teaspoon agave nectar or yacon

1 lemon wedge   syrup (optional)

Push all of the ingredients through the hopper of a juicer with the apple. Alternatively, combine all the ingredients in a high-powered blender, and process on high until smooth. Serve thoroughly chilled.

Rich Milk Shake ....

This is a very satisfying meal when you do not have much time to chew.

2 to 3 cups apple juice

1 cup raw Brazil nuts (soaked)

2 frozen bananas

1 tablespoon Raw Almond Butter
(page 160)

½ teaspoon ground cinnamon

Combine all the ingredients in a high-powered blender, and process until smooth. Serve immediately.

Sesame Milk .... YIELD: 5 TO 7 SERVINGS

This milk is rich in calcium and is suitable as a breakfast drink or as a midafternoon energy booster.

3 to 5 cups chilled water

2 cups soaked raw sesame seeds

4 to 6 tablespoons agave nectar

¼ teaspoon fresh vanilla seeds
(scraped from a vanilla bean)

Combine the water and sesame seeds in a high-powered blender, and process until smooth and creamy. Strain through a nut milk bag or cheesecloth. Return the milk to the blender, and add the remaining ingredients. Process briefly on low. Serve at room temperature or thoroughly chilled.

NOTE: This milk can be used in most of the recipes in this book that call for cashew or almond milk.

Star Fruit Shake .... YIELD : 3 CUPS

1 to 2 cups water

¾ cup Cashew Milk (page 40)

½ cup coconut flesh

4 to 6 pitted medjool dates

1 large, very ripe star fruit

Combine the water, milk, coconut, and dates in a high-powered blender, and process on high until smooth. Cut the star fruit into pieces and add it to the blender. Process just until the desired texture is achieved. Serve immediately or thoroughly chilled.

Green Strawberry Drink .... YIELD: ABOUT 2 TO 3 SERVINGS

This makes a very tasty and highly nutritious meal.

1 bunch spinach

2 Granny Smith apples, quartered

10 to 12 strawberries, stems removed

Bunch up the spinach and push the it and the strawberries through the hopper of a juicer with the apples. Alternatively, combine all the ingredients in a high-powered blender with a little water, and process until smooth. Serve immediately.

Summer Delight .... YIELD: 2 TO 3 SERVINGS

This drink will help prevent overheating and dehydration. It can be served on a hot summer day as a replacement for a heavier meal.

½ small watermelon

Thoroughly wash the skin of the watermelon. Cut the melon into vertical strips, and put it through the hopper of a juicer. Alternatively, remove the skin, add more of the red flesh, remove the seeds, if you prefer, and process the melon in a high-powered blender until smooth. Serve in chilled glasses.

Summer Drink .... YIELD: 3 TO 4 CUPS

½ pineapple, peeled and chopped

2 cups apple juice

1 mint sprig

Combine all the ingredients in a high-powered blender, and process until smooth. Serve thoroughly chilled.

NOTE: If you prefer to process the pineapple through a juicer, it does not need to be peeled.

Summer Quencher .... YIELD: 1 SERVING

2 apples, quartered

1 small handful fresh spearmint

1 celery stalk

½ lemon, cut into wedges

Wrap the spearmint leaves around pieces of the apple and push through the hopper of a juicer with the celery and lemon wedges. Alternatively, juice the lemon and place the juice and remaining ingredients in a high-powered blender. Add a little chilled water, and process on high until smooth. Serve thoroughly chilled.

Tropical Fruit Punch .... YIELD: 1 SERVING

½ cup chopped papaya

1 orange, peeled and quartered

1 frozen or fresh banana

¼ cup pineapple cubes

¼ cup ice

1 to 2 tablespoons agave nectar,
  or 3 to 5 pitted dates, sliced

¼ teaspoon freshly squeezed lime
  juice (optional)

Place the papaya in a high-powered blender, then add the remaining ingredients. Process for about 60 seconds, or until completely smooth. Serve immediately.

NOTE: Using a frozen banana will make a thicker shake.

Tropical Milk Shake .... YIELD: ABOUT 2 CUPS

1 young Thai coconut, water and flesh

1 cup raw macadamia nuts

1 frozen banana

½ cup pineapple cubes

4 or 5 ice cubes

4 or 5 pitted dates

Dash of freshly squeezed lime juice

Combine all the ingredients in a high-powered blender, and process on high until smooth and creamy. Serve immediately.

Vanilla Milk Shake ....

This is a great after-school drink for children.

2 to 3 cups Almond Milk (page 34)

1 young Thai coconut, water and flesh

3 to 4 ice cubes (optional)

2 to 3 pitted dates

1 vanilla bean, scraped

Combine all the ingredients in a high-powered blender, and process on high until smooth and creamy. Serve immediately.

Gary's Green Smoothie .... YIELD : 1 TO 2 SERVINGS

This is an extremely delicious way to get more greens into your daily diet.

1 young Thai coconut, water and flesh

½ bunch cilantro

½ bunch Italian parsley

1 to 2 black kale leaves

¼ to ½ cup palm nectar

1 slice (¼ inch thick) red jalapeño chile

1 small garlic clove

Combine all the ingredients in a high-powered blender, and process for about 1 minutes, or until fluid and smooth. Serve immediately.

Salads and Dressings

In raw vegan cuisine, salads are very simple and extremely creative and tasty. The recipes in this chapter will probably be the most familiar to people who are used to cooked foods. Because I have noticed that a majority of my clients and students get into a rut and eat the same foods over and over, I have chosen some of the less-used vegetables and fruits so that you will be enticed to add variety to your diet.

Artichoke Salad .... YIELD: 3 TO 4 SERVINGS

12 artichokes, stems removed

2 lemons, juiced

1 bunch basil, chopped

1 bunch mint, chopped

1 tablespoon raw apple cider vinegar

1 to 2 bay leaves

2 garlic cloves

Dash of Celtic sea salt

Dash of cayenne

2 to 3 tablespoons raw olive oil

Cut the artichoke hearts into pieces and place in a bowl. Combine the juice of $1\frac{1}{2}$ of the lemons and the basil, vinegar, mint, bay leaves, garlic, salt, and cayenne in a high-powered blender, and process on low. Drizzle in the olive oil and blend again. Adjust the salt and cayenne seasonings, if necessary. Pour over the artichoke hearts along with the remaining lemon juice. Let marinate for 2 to 3 hours before serving.

NOTE: If this salad tastes too "raw" to you, marinate it longer (for 8 to 12 hours) or place it in a dehydrator at 105 degrees F for 4 to 6 hours before serving. For a warming winter dish, choose the latter option. You can also combine these two techniques. Marinate the salad for 8 to 12 hours, and then place it in the dehydrator for a few hours, checking for the desired texture from time to time.

Asparagus and Orange Salad

8 ounces asparagus, trimmed and cut into 2-inch pieces

2 oranges

2 ripe tomatoes, cut into 8 wedges

2 ounces romaine lettuce leaves, shredded

2 tablespoons raw olive oil

½ teaspoon umeboshi vinegar

Dash of Celtic sea salt

Dash of cayenne

Place the asparagus in a serving bowl or on a platter. Grate the peel from half of one of the orange and put it aside. Peel both oranges and cut them into segments, without the membrane. Squeeze out the juice from the membrane and set it aside.

Place the orange segments, tomatoes, and lettuce in the bowl with the asparagus. Combine the oil and vinegar in a small bowl, and add 1 tablespoon of the reserved orange juice and 1 teaspoon of the grated peel. Season with the salt and cayenne to taste; if this is being served as a winter dish, add extra cayenne. Just before serving, pour the dressing over the salad and toss gently to coat.

Asparagus with Citrus-Ginger Sauce

YIELD: 3 TO 4 SERVINGS

2 to 3 pounds asparagus

1 tablespoon umeboshi vinegar or raw apple cider vinegar

1 tablespoon freshly squeezed orange juice

1 tablespoon grated orange peel

1½ teaspoons grated fresh ginger

1 teaspoon Nama Shoyu

1 garlic clove, crushed

½ teaspoon agave nectar (optional)

½ teaspoon raw brown mustard seeds

Dash of ground cardamom

Dash of Celtic sea salt

Mixed baby greens or sprouted micro greens

10 to 12 cherry tomatoes

Snap off the tough ends of the asparagus and peel the stalks, if desired. Place the asparagus in a large serving bowl. Combine the vinegar, orange juice, grated peel, ginger, Nama Shoyu, garlic, optional agave nectar, mustard seeds, cardamom, and salt in a high-powered blender, and process until mixed. Pour over the asparagus and allow to marinate for 8 to 12 hours in the refrigerator. Alternatively, place the asparagus and marinade in a dehydrator at 105 to 108 degrees F until the desired texture and tenderness is achieved. Serve on a bed of mixed baby greens, and garnish with the cherry tomatoes.

Avocado-Watercress Salad ...... Yield: 4 servings

2 ripe avocados, cut in half, pits removed

1 tablespoon Vegan Herb Mayonnaise (page 167)

1 teaspoon agave nectar or stevia powder or liquid

1 tablespoon Raw Mustard (page 160)

1 teaspoon umeboshi vinegar

2 large bunches watercress

1 red bell pepper, sliced

1 Cox's apple, cored and diced

Place the avocado halves on a serving dish. Combine the mayonnaise, agave nectar, mustard, and vinegar in bowl, and stir until well blended. Chop the watercress and put it in a salad bowl with the bell pepper and apple. Add the mayonnaise mixture and mix well. Put this mixture in each of the avocado halves and serve.

Colorful Watercress Salad .... Yield: 4 to 5 servings

2 large bunches watercress

⅓ cup raw pine nuts

3 bell peppers (red, yellow, and orange), coarsely chopped

1 zucchini, coarsely chopped

1 Granny Smith apple, grated

8 to 10 cherry tomatoes, halved

1 red onion, diced

1 tablespoon raw olive or hemp oil

1 tablespoon soft raw hempseeds (optional)

1 tablespoon raw apple cider vinegar

⅓ teaspoon umeboshi vinegar

Dash of Celtic sea salt

Dash of cayenne

Combine all the ingredients in a large salad bowl and toss well. Adjust the seasonings, if necessary.

Cheezy Cruciferous Salad ...... YIELD: 4 TO 5 SERVINGS

1 head broccoli, cut into bite-size
florets

1 head cauliflower, cut into bite-size
florets

½ cup raw cashews

¼ cup water

¼ cup freshly squeezed lemon juice

1 red bell pepper, coarsely chopped

2 tablespoons Nama Shoyu,
or 1 teaspoon Celtic sea salt

Place the broccoli and cauliflowers in a bowl. Combine the cashews, water, and lemon juice in a high-powered blender, and process until smooth. Add the bell pepper and Nama Shoyu, and process again until smooth. Pour over the broccoli and cauliflower.

NOTE: This dish can be made in advance; the dressing will help soften the vegetables.

Cruciferous Vegetables in Teriyaki Sauce .... YIELD: 6 TO 8 SERVINGS

1 head cauliflower, cut into bite-size
florets

1 head broccoli, cut into bite-size
florets

1 lemon, juiced

Celtic sea salt, to taste

2 tablespoons Teriyaki Sauce
(page 166)

Place the cauliflower and broccoli in a large bowl, and sprinkle with the lemon juice and salt, mixing well to make sure they are evenly distributed. Pour the Teriyaki Sauce over the broccoli and cauliflower and mix well, making sure it is evenly distributed. Adjust the amount of sauce according to your desired taste. Let marinate until serving time.

NOTE: The longer this marinates, the softer the vegetables will become.

Curried Spinach-Apple Salad

The addition of sauerkraut enhances the healing qualities of this recipe, so be sure to make it often.

2 to 3 cups chopped spinach

1 cup Vegan Herb Mayonnaise
(page 167)

2 teaspoons curry powder

2 cups raw sauerkraut, with liquid

1 large, unpeeled apple, finely diced

¾ cup raw chutney (use any of the
recipes from this book)

¾ cup raw pistachios, chopped

Combine the spinach, mayonnaise, and curry powder in a large mixing bowl. Add the sauerkraut, apple, chutney, and pistachios, and mix well. Chill thoroughly before serving.

Almond and Pear Salad ...... YIELD: 3 TO 4 SERVINGS

This recipe is good for preteens and teenagers who wish to develop gourmet food preparation skills.

2 cups cubed zucchini

½ red bell pepper, sliced lengthwise

¼ cup diced celery

¼ teaspoon Celtic sea salt

½ cup Cashew Milk (page 40)

2 tablespoons Vegan Herb
Mayonnaise (page 167)

½ teaspoon Raw Mustard (page 160)

¼ teaspoon ground ginger

2 Comice, Anjou, or Bosc pears, cored
and cut into 1-inch cubes

1 head lettuce

2 tablespoons slivered raw almonds

Toss the zucchini, bell pepper, and celery together in a large mixing bowl. Sprinkle with the salt. Add the cashew milk, mayonnaise, mustard, and ginger, and mix well. Gently mix in the pears. Line individual salad plates with the lettuce leaves, and arrange the salad on top. Sprinkle with the almonds just before serving.

Party Oriental Pear Salad

YIELD: ABOUT 30 TO 32 SERVINGS

This is a great way for preteens and teenagers to consume greens while at a party.

3 heads romaine lettuce, shredded

8 green Anjou pears, cored and sliced

2 cups diagonally sliced red bell peppers

2 cups sliced green onions

½ cup raw sesame seeds

Sesame Oil Dressing (page 64)

Toss the lettuce, pears, red bell peppers, and the green onions in an extra-large mixing bowl. (You might need to use two large mixing bowls.) Add the sesame seeds, and toss again. Serve with the dressing.

Sesame Oil Dressing .... YIELD: ABOUT 1 QUART

This is a very tasty dressing for Party Oriental Pear Salad (page 64).

2 cups raw apple cider vinegar

1 cup raw sesame oil

¾ cup Nama Shoyu

2¼ tablespoons agave nectar or yacon syrup

1 teaspoon crushed red chile flakes (optional)

Combine all the ingredients in a high-powered blender, and process on low speed.

Cucumber Salad .... YIELD: 4 TO 5 SERVINGS

4 young cucumbers, thickly sliced

4 celery stalks, thinly sliced

2 carrots, thinly sliced

¾ cup umeboshi vinegar

⅓ cup stevia powder or liquid or
   agave nectar

1 tablespoon raw olive oil

1½ teaspoons Celtic sea salt

2 green onions, sliced

2 stalks fresh dill, finely chopped
   (optional)

Place the cucumbers, carrots, and celery in a serving bowl. Combine the vinegar, stevia, oil, and salt in a bottle. Seal the bottle, and shake well. Pour over the vegetables, and garnish with the green onions and dill. Marinate in the refrigerator for a minimum of 1 to 2 hours before serving.

NOTE: If you find that slicing the vegetables by hand is too labor intensive, use a mandoline or spiral slicer (see page 18).

Cucumber-Radish Salad .... YIELD: 4 TO 5 SERVINGS

2 cucumbers, cut in half lengthwise
   and sliced into half-moons

1 bunch radishes, cut in half and sliced
   into half-moons

8 ounces water chestnuts, sliced into
   half-moons (optional)

1 tablespoon umeboshi vinegar or raw
   apple cider vinegar

1 tablespoon raw Asian dark sesame
   oil

1 teaspoon agave nectar, stevia
   powder or liquid, or yacon syrup
   (optional)

½ teaspoon Celtic sea salt, more or
   less to taste

Toss the cucumbers, radishes, and water chestnuts together in a large bowl. Whisk the vinegar, oil, optional agave nectar, and salt in a small bowl. Pour a small amount of this dressing over the vegetables and toss. Adjust the amount of dressing to your taste.

Dandelion Greens Salad ...... YIELD: 6 TO 8 SERVINGS

1 bunch dandelion greens

4 carrots, shredded

3 to 4 cucumbers, cubed

3 to 4 Red Delicious apples, cubed

3 ripe avocados, cubed

1 Gala or Fuji apple, grated

1 beet, shredded

12 cherry tomatoes, cut in half

¼ cup raw olive oil or hemp oil

6 to 8 pitted raw olives, quartered

2 tablespoons raw capers (optional)

1 lemon, juiced

1 tablespoon umeboshi vinegar or raw apple cider vinegar

1 teaspoon Celtic sea salt

½ teaspoon cayenne

Dash of turmeric

Chop or tear the dandelion greens into small pieces, and place in a bowl. Add the carrots, cucumbers, avocados, apple, beet, and cherry tomatoes. Mix thoroughly. Add the oil, olives, optional capers, lemon juice, vinegar, salt, cayenne, and turmeric. Mix well. Refrigerate for 20 to 30 minutes before serving to blend the flavors.

NOTE: If you find the taste of the dandelion greens to be too bitter, marinate them in Marinade Sauce (page 157) for 2 to 4 hours before adding the other ingredients.

Grapefruit Salad .... YIELD: 5 TO 6 SERVINGS

2 ruby red grapefruits, peeled and separated into segments

1 head lettuce, shredded

1 ripe avocado, diced

4 green onions, thinly sliced (optional)

3 tablespoons raw grapeseed oil

1 tablespoon raw apple cider vinegar

⅛ teaspoon ground cinnamon

Celtic sea salt, to taste

Place the grapefruit segments, lettuce, avocado, and green onions in a bowl. Whisk together the oil, vinegar, cinnamon, and salt in a small bowl. Pour over the salad, toss gently, and serve.

Dinner Salad with Truffle Oil Dressing

YIELD: 6 SERVINGS

6 to 8 cups mixed salad greens

2 tart Braeburn or Jonathan apples, cut into thin wedges or strips

1 turnip (peeling is optional), cut into thin strips

2 tablespoons chopped raw walnuts

¼ cup umeboshi vinegar

2 tablespoons raw truffle oil

2 tablespoons freshly squeezed lemon juice

2 tablespoons rapadura or stevia powder or liquid (optional)

¼ to ½ teaspoon cayenne

Dash of Celtic sea salt

Divide the salad greens among 6 plates. Arrange the apples and turnip over the greens. Sprinkle the walnuts on top. Combine the vinegar, oil, lemon juice, rapadura, cayenne, and salt in a jar. Seal the jar, and shake until well blended. Drizzle about 1 tablespoon of this dressing over each plate of salad. Serve as soon as possible to prevent the lettuce from wilting. Refrigerate any remaining dressing.

Bunny Salad .... YIELD: 1 TO 2 SERVINGS

This is a fun salad for all ages, but it is ideal to make with preschoolers.

1 medium pear, cored and cut in half

¼ teaspoon freshly squeezed lemon juice

4 raisins or mulberries

2 large almonds, sliced in half

12 thin strips carrot

3 to 5 goji berries

Dip the cut side of the pear in the lemon juice. Place the pear halves on a serving plate, cut-side down. Decorate the top end of each half with 2 raisins for the eyes, the almond halves for the ears, 6 carrot strips for whiskers, and the goji berries for the nose and tail.

NOTE: This is meant to be a fun project to do with young children, so you will need to do the prep work and allow the children to assemble the bunnies themselves.

Winter Pear Salad ....

1 cup chopped spinach

1 cup chopped lettuce

½ cup sliced mushrooms

½ cup bean sprouts

¼ cup sliced radishes

1 Anjou or Bosc pear, chopped

1 teaspoon Ground Lemon Peel
  (page 169)

Winter Pear Salad Dressing (below)

Combine the spinach, lettuce, mushrooms, sprouts, and radishes in a salad bowl. Toss with large salad spoons. Add the pears and lemon peel and toss again. Toss with the dressing and serve.

Winter Pear Salad Dressing

YIELD: ½ CUP

Pour this dressing over Winter Pear Salad (above) or any other salad of your choice.

1 Seckel or Anjou pear, chopped

3 tablespoons raw olive oil or
  grapeseed oil

1 tablespoon raw apple cider vinegar

1 tablespoon freshly squeezed lemon
  juice

1½ teaspoons freshly squeezed
  orange juice

½ teaspoon Celtic sea salt

Combine all the ingredients in a high-powered blender, and process until smooth and well blended. Serve immediately.

Kimchee ....

This is a very popular fermented food staple in Korea. The Great Wall of China was reported to be built on brown rice and kimchee. Serve it as a salad, condiment, or relish. The smell can be quite pungent and the taste is strong.

3 pounds napa cabbage

3 tablespoons coarse Celtic sea salt or Himalayan salt

¾ cup shredded carrots

½ pound daikon radish, shredded

5 large garlic cloves, minced

1 large red bell pepper, cut into matchsticks

2 tablespoons crushed red chile flakes

¼ cup Nama Shoyu

¼ cup grated fresh ginger

1 tablespoon umeboshi vinegar

1 tablespoon stevia powder or liquid

8 green onions, finely chopped

1 teaspoon raw sesame oil

Chop the cabbage into 1-inch pieces, and place it in a glass or nonreactive bowl. Sprinkle with 2 tablespoons of the salt and let stand for 3 to 4 hours, until the cabbage is wilted by half its volume. Rinse the cabbage in cold water and drain off any liquid. Add all the remaining ingredients, except the sesame oil, and mix well. Transfer to a glass jar, Mason jar, or ceramic crock (do not use plastic!), and press down until the cabbage is submerged in liquid. Cover with food-grade plastic wrap, and add a weight to keep it down, if necessary. Allow the cabbage to stand at room temperature for 1 to 4 days (the amount of time needed will depend on the temperature in the room; make sure the temperature is not above 80 degrees F). Refrigerate. Sprinkle with the sesame oil before serving.

NOTE: Fermentation makes food easier to digest and the nutrients easier to assimilate.

Cultured Vegetables .... YIELD: 6 TO 8 SERVINGS

Although this fermented salad will probably last for months, it is best to take advantage of all the enzymes and friendly bacteria by consuming it within two weeks.

2 heads green cabbage

1 head purple cabbage

1 thumb-size piece of ginger, unpeeled

1 head cauliflower, chopped

1 bunch fresh dill, chopped

1 cup freshly squeezed lemon juice

1 tablespoon Celtic sea salt

Push 2½ heads of the cabbage and the ginger through the hopper of a juicer. Place both the pulp and juice in a medium mixing bowl. Take off the outer layers of the remaining cabbage and set aside. Chop the rest of the cabbage and add it to the bowl along with the cauliflower, dill, lemon juice, and salt. Mix well.

Transfer to a ceramic crock, and cover with 2 layers of the reserved cabbage leaves. Cover this with a plate that is large enough to almost cover the crock. Place a 16-ounce jar filled with water on top of the plate. Cover this with a dish towel, and let rest at room temperature (not above 70 degrees F) for about 5 days.

If you see any mold when you remove the cover, simply scoop off the top layer and discard it. Place the mixture in airtight glass jars and store in the refrigerator.

Marinated Mustard Coleslaw

1 head green cabbage, shredded

3 carrots, grated

1 cup raw mustard oil, or 1 teaspoon raw mustard seeds

¾ cup raw apple cider vinegar

¾ teaspoon umeboshi plum, crushed into a paste

1 teaspoon Celtic sea salt

½ cup stevia powder, or ½ cup agave nectar or yacon syrup

Put the cabbage and carrots in a large salad bowl. Place the oil, vinegar, umeboshi plum, and salt in a high-powered blender, and process until well combined. Sweeten gradually with stevia to taste. Blend again and pour into the bowl over the cabbage and carrots. Mix thoroughly, and marinate for several hours before serving.

Pear and Mixed Green Salad

3 pears

3 tablespoons freshly squeezed lemon juice

6 ounces mixed salad greens

½ cup raw hazelnuts, soaked and dehydrated

2 tablespoons raw hazelnut oil or walnut oil

1 tablespoon raw apple cider vinegar

1 teaspoon Dijon mustard

¼ teaspoon Celtic sea salt, or to taste

Peel, core, and slice the pears, and toss them with the lemon juice. Arrange the salad greens on 2 serving plates, then place the pears on top. Chop the hazelnuts and sprinkle them on the salad. To make a dressing, whisk the oil, vinegar, and mustard in a bowl. Add the salt to taste. Spoon the dressing over the salad and serve immediately.

Very Green Mesclun Salad
with Tahini Dressing

1 cup mesclun

1 cup watercress

1 cup arugula

1 cup red and green chicory, more or less to taste

1 cup Japanese mustard greens

1 garlic clove, smashed

1 1/2 teaspoons coarse Celtic sea salt

2 lemons, juiced

2 tablespoons raw tahini

1 1/2 teaspoons agave nectar or stevia powder or liquid

1/2 teaspoon cayenne

1/2 cup raw olive oil

1 teaspoon chopped fresh spearmint

1 teaspoon chopped fresh tarragon

Wash the mesclun, watercress, arugula, chicory, and mustard greens, and set aside.

Rub the inside of a large wooden salad bowl with the smashed garlic clove and 1 tablespoon of the salt. Then mince the garlic and place it in the bowl along with the lemon juice, the remaining 1 1/2 teaspoons salt, and the tahini, agave nectar, and cayenne. Gradually whisk in the oil. Add the greens and toss well, until they are evenly coated. Garnish with the mint and tarragon and serve.

Pepper Leaf Salad with Chili Dressing

YIELD: 2 SERVINGS

1 head radicchio, coarsely chopped

2 to 4 cucumbers, diced

2 red bell peppers, chopped

1 star fruit, sliced

6 ounces watercress, coarsely chopped

4 ounces Cape gooseberries (if available)

2 ounces arugula

6 green onions, sliced

Chili Dressing (below)

Combine the radicchio, cucumbers, bell peppers, star fruit, watercress, Cape gooseberries, arugula, and green onions in a large salad bowl. Add the dressing and toss until all the ingredients are evenly coated.

Chili Dressing .... YIELD: 2 SERVINGS

2 tablespoons raw olive oil

1 tablespoon raw chili oil

1 tablespoon raw mustard oil

1 teaspoon agave nectar or stevia powder or liquid (optional)

1 garlic clove

1 teaspoon Celtic sea salt

Dash of ground cinnamon

Combine all the ingredients in a high-powered blender. Adjust the salt and cinnamon to taste.

NOTE: This is a very warming salad dressing that is great during cold winters.

Quick Salad .... Yield: 2 to 3 servings

2 lemons

1 bag (5 to 8 ounces) prewashed mixed baby greens

1 to 2 packages (1.75 ounces each) sprouted micro greens

1 cup shredded beets

1 cup shredded carrots

1¼ cup raw olive oil

1 teaspoon ground cinnamon, more or less to taste

Dash of Celtic sea salt

Cut the ends off the lemons. Thinly slice the rest of the unpeeled lemons and put them in a large salad bowl. Place all the vegetables in the bowl and toss well. Add the olive oil and season with the cinnamon and salt to taste. Toss again and serve.

Quick Summer Salad .... Yield: 5 to 6 servings

¾ cup umeboshi vinegar

⅓ cup stevia powder or liquid (optional)

1½ teaspoons Celtic sea salt

7 to 9 cucumbers, thinly sliced with a mandoline

2 carrots, shredded

4 celery stalks, thinly sliced

2 green onions, sliced

2 stalks fresh dill

Combine the vinegar, stevia, and salt, and adjust to the desired taste. Place the cucumbers, carrots, and celery in a bowl, add the vinegar mixture, and refrigerate for 1 to 2 hours. Garnish with the green onions and dill just before serving.

Quick Watercress Salad with Dressing

YIELD: 2 SERVINGS

3 ounces watercress

8 to 10 cherry tomatoes, cut in half

5 to 6 cucumbers, cubed

1 tablespoon organic brown mustard seeds

1 garlic clove

3 tablespoons raw walnut oil, hemp oil, or olive oil

1 tablespoon umeboshi vinegar

1 teaspoon cayenne

¼ teaspoon Celtic sea salt

Mince or tear the watercress into small pieces in a salad bowl. Add the cherry tomatoes and cucumbers, and toss gently until evenly distributed.

Place the mustard seeds and garlic in a mortar and grind with a pestle. Transfer to a high-powered blender and add the oil, vinegar, cayenne, and salt. Process until well combine. Pour over the salad, and toss until the vegetables are evenly coated.

Seaweed-Cucumber Salad ....YIELD: 2 SERVINGS

Serve this salad in the summer for the extra nourishment obtained from sea vegetables.

2 cucumbers (preferably the Orient Express variety)

1 cup raw dulse or arame, soaked and drained

¼ cup raw sesame oil or grapeseed oil

1 tablespoon Nama Shoyu

⅛ cup umeboshi vinegar

1 teaspoon stevia powder or agave nectar (optional)

Dash of cayenne

Dash of ground ginger

Slice the cucumbers thinly using a mandoline or spiral slicer (see page 18). Place the cucumber slices in a medium glass salad bowl along with the drained arame. Add the remaining ingredients and mix well. Marinate for 2 to 4 hours in refrigerator before serving. Serve thoroughly chilled.

Spicy Corn Salad .... YIELD: 4 SERVINGS

2 cups raw corn kernels

¾ cup chopped red bell peppers

½ cup chopped green onions

¼ cup chopped fresh cilantro

5 to 8 pitted raw green olives, chopped

2 tablespoons freshly squeezed lemon juice

2 tablespoons raw mustard oil

1 red jalapeño chile, seeded and finely minced

1 to 2 teaspoons Celtic sea salt

½ teaspoon ground cumin

Raw salad greens, or 2 ripe avocados (optional)

Combine the corn, bell peppers, green onions, cilantro, olives, lemon juice, mustard oil, chile, salt, and cumin in a bowl, and toss until evenly combined. Serve as is, or on a bed of raw salad greens or in pitted avocado halves.

Marinated Mushrooms .... YIELD: 2 SERVINGS

Serve this dish on a bed of butter lettuce and green sprouts.

2 portobello mushrooms, chopped

2 tablespoons raw olive oil

½ teaspoon Celtic sea salt

Dash of cayenne

Dash of freshly squeezed lemon juice

Combine all the ingredients in a bowl and mix well. Allow to marinate for 8 to 12 hours. Alternatively, place in a dehydrator for 1 hour at 105 degrees F.

Sprouts Fiesta ....

2 to 3 cups clover sprouts

1 cup daikon sprouts (optional)

1 cup sunflower sprouts

1 cup mung bean sprouts

1 cup bean sprouts

4 to 5 ripe avocados, cubed

1 red jalapeño chile, finely diced

½ cup raw olive oil

¼ cup freshly squeezed lemon juice

2 tablespoons Nama Shoyu

1 shallot, finely diced

1½ teaspoons freshly squeezed lime juice

½ teaspoon Jamaican curry powder

¼ teaspoon curry powder

¼ teaspoon Italian seasoning

½ purple onion, finely diced

2 to 4 green onions, thinly sliced

1 ripe avocado, mashed

Combine all of the sprouts, the cubed avocado, and chile in a bowl. Place the olive oil, lemon juice, Nama Shoyu, shallot, lime juice, Jamaican curry powder, curry powder, and Italian seasoning in a high-powered blender, and process until well combined. Pour over the sprouts. Add the purple onion, green onions, and mashed avocado. Mix thoroughly. Marinate in the refrigerator for about 30 minutes before serving.

Sweet-and-Tart Dandelion Salad

This is most tasty when it is served with Sweet Almond Dressing (below).

2 bunches dandelion greens, chopped

2 bunches collard greens, chopped

1 cup shredded Granny Smith apples

1 cup raisins

1/2 cup diced red cabbage

1 onion, finely diced

Sweet dressing of your choice

Combine the greens, apples, raisins, cabbage, and onion in a salad bowl and mix well. Serve with any sweet dressing of your choice.

Sweet Almond Dressing .... YIELD: 1 CUP

This is a great dressing for bitter greens, such as those in the Sweet-and-Tart Dandelion Salad (above).

¾ cup raw olive oil, hemp oil, or flaxseed oil

2 to 4 tablespoons Raw Almond Butter (page 160)

2 to 3 tablespoons agave nectar or yacon syrup

2 tablespoons umeboshi vinegar

2 tablespoons Nama Shoyu

¼ teaspoon cayenne

Place all the ingredients in a high-powered blender, and process until well combined. To use, pour over the salad, toss, and let marinate for 2 to 4 hours before serving.

Thanksgiving Salad

This autumn or winter holiday meal is a quick, easy, and familiar way to introduce family and friends to raw vegan cuisine.

3 medium persimmons

3 cups baby spinach

¼ cup raw pecans, soaked and dehydrated

¼ cup dried cranberries or dried cherries

Thanksgiving Salad Dressing (below) or Sweet Almond Dressing (page 78)

Remove the stems of the persimmons, cut the fruit in half, and scoop out the flesh with a spoon or cut it into vertical slices and peel off the skin. Place in a large salad bowl, add the remaining ingredients, and toss. Pour a generous amount of the dressing over the salad. Toss again and serve.

Thanksgiving Salad Dressing

3 tablespoons freshly squeezed orange juice

3 tablespoons raw olive oil

2 tablespoons raw apple cider vinegar

1 garlic clove, crushed

½ teaspoon Celtic sea salt

¼ teaspoon cayenne

Combine all the ingredients in a high-powered blender, and process until smooth and well blended. Chill thoroughly before serving.

Thai Goddess Dressing .... YIELD: 1½ CUPS

¾ cup water

¼ cups cashews, soaked

3 tablespoons freshly squeezed lime juice

2 tablespoons sliced green onions

1 tablespoon unpasteurized raw golden miso

1 teaspoon minced fresh ginger

1 teaspoon stevia powder

¼ teaspoon crushed red chile flakes

Combine all the ingredients in a high-powered blender or a food processor fitted with the S blade, and process until smooth and creamy. If necessary, blend in batches or add water sparingly to thin.

Tahini-Mint Dressing .... YIELD: 1 CUP

1 cup fresh peppermint leaves

1 very ripe avocado (optional)

¼ cup raw tahini

¼ cup water

3 tablespoons freshly squeezed lemon juice

1 garlic clove, minced

Dash of Flower of the Ocean sea minerals

Combine the peppermint, optional avocado, tahini, water, lemon juice, and garlic in a high-powered blender, and process until smooth. Stop and scrape down the sides of the blender jar as necessary. Add the sea minerals to taste. Store in an airtight container in the refrigerator.

Watercress Citrus Salad .... Yield: 2 servings

1 pink grapefruit, peeled, seeded, and thinly sliced

1 orange, peeled, seeded, and thinly sliced

13 ounces watercress

1 Cox's apple, cored and diced

2 ounces sultanas

Sweet Almond Dressing (page 78) or other fruity dressing of your choice

Divide the grapefruit and orange slices among 4 plates. Arrange the watercress on top of the fruit. Combine the apple and sultanas, and scatter over the watercress. Serve with the dressing on the side.

Arugula Salad .... Yield: 1 serving

1 cup arugula

1 tangerine, peeled, seeded, and separated into segments

1 tablespoon soft raw hempseeds

1 tablespoon Incan berries

1 teaspoon mulberries

1 teaspoon raw capers (optional)

Sweet Almond Dressing (page 78) or Pineapple Dressing (page 83)

Place the arugula, tangerine, hemp, Incan berries, mulberries, and optional capers in a small bowl, and toss until well combined. Serve with the dressing of your choice.

Creamy Dressing ....

This is great for salads, as a dip for crudités, or served over bitter greens.

- 1 ripe avocado
- 1 tomato, chopped
- 1 rose geranium leaf (optional, but makes a big difference)
- Fresh dill, to taste
- Dash of Celtic sea salt
- 1 cup carrot juice
- 2 teaspoons raisins (optional)

Combine the avocado, tomato, optional rose geranium leaf, dill, and salt in a high-powered blender, and process on low to medium speed, pouring in the carrot juice at intervals until the desired thickness is achieved. Add the raisins, if using, and blend again.

NOTE: You can make this dressing in advance and store it in the refrigerator.

Avocado Dressing .... YIELD: ABOUT 1 CUP

Use this dressing on salads or as a sauce or dip.

- 1 ripe avocado, diced
- 1 cucumber, chopped
- 1 cup chopped watercress
- 1 handful fresh dill, chopped
- 1 teaspoon Atlantic kelp powder
- 1 teaspoon cayenne
- ½ teaspoon Flower of the Ocean sea minerals
- 1 tablespoon raw capers

Combine the avocado, cucumber, watercress, dill, kelp, cayenne, and sea minerals in a bowl, and mix well. Add the capers just before serving. Adjust the seasonings to taste.

East Indian Dressing ....

The spices in this dressing are known for their immunity-boosting properties and are therefore recommended for regular use in the winter months.

2 cups raw olive oil or mustard oil

2 tablespoons turmeric

2 tablespoons ground fennel

1 tablespoon ground cumin

1 tablespoon ground coriander

1 teaspoon ground ginger

½ teaspoon crushed red chile flakes

½ teaspoon cayenne

¼ teaspoon ground cinnamon

Dash of freshly squeezed lemon juice

Combine all the ingredients in a bottle. Seal tightly and shake well before serving.

Pineapple Dressing .... YIELD: 2 CUPS

Pour this dressing over a vegetable salad, or use it as a dipping sauce for crudités.

1 cup diced pineapple

¾ cup raw flaxseed oil or olive oil

2 tablespoons Dijon mustard

1 lime, juiced

1 tablespoon Celtic sea salt

½ teaspoon raw apple cider vinegar

1 garlic clove, crushed

Combine all the ingredients in a high-powered blender, and process until smooth.

Walnut Vinaigrette ....

This salad dressing is particularly well suited for holiday entertaining.

⅓ cup freshly squeezed orange juice

¼ cup raw walnut oil

¼ cup raw grapeseed oil

3 tablespoons raw apple cider vinegar

2 to 4 tablespoons celery juice

2 tablespoons finely chopped raw walnuts

2 tablespoons Raw Mustard (page 160; optional)

1 shallot, finely chopped

Dash of Flower of the Ocean sea minerals

Dash of cayenne

Combine all the ingredients in a high-powered blender, and process until smooth and well blended. Chill thoroughly before serving.

Soups

The recipes in this section are fresh and exciting. For those who think raw soups could not possibly be tasty, think of the times you ate borscht or gazpacho and never realized that they were raw. Soup is one of the most enjoyable ways to eat raw food, and many people who are new to raw vegan cuisine are surprised at how satisfying and delicious raw soup can be.

In the winter months, a warm soup may be desired. Raw soups can be warmed by putting them in direct sunlight or in a dehydrator at 105 degrees F (or higher) for several hours.

Basic Soup Broth ....

8 to 10 cups water

5 to 6 celery stalks

4 to 6 carrots

3 to 4 zucchinis

1 to 2 beets

1 to 2 red potatoes

2 to 3 tablespoons umeboshi vinegar

½ onion

3 to 4 tablespoons Nama Shoyu

1 thyme sprig

½ mint stalk

Combine all the ingredients in a high-powered blender, and process until the desired consistency is achieved.

VARIATION—THIN VEGETABLE BROTH: For a thinner broth, use a juicer to extract the juice from the celery, carrots, zucchinis, beets, and potatoes. Put the juice into a high-powered blender. Reduce the water to 2 to 3 cups and add it to the blender along with the remaining ingredients. Blend thoroughly.

NOTES: This is a great aid for those who lack stamina or desire a strengthening liquid.

• If you have been on a cleanse or fast, this is a very quick and easy way to reintroduce nourishment into the body. Make sure to only drink small amounts at a time until your body has acclimatized to food again.

Broccoli Soup ....

6 cups water, or more as needed

2 to 4 cups chopped broccoli

2 cups raw cashews

1 ripe avocado

½ cup fresh cilantro

¼ cup chopped onions

1 tablespoon Nama Shoyu, more or less to taste

½ teaspoon ground cinnamon

1 tablespoon raw hemp oil (optional)

Combine the water, broccoli, cashews, avocado, cilantro, onions, Nama Shoyu, and cinnamon in a high-powered blender, and process until smooth. Add more water or broccoli to achieve the desired consistency. Adjust the amount of Nama Shoyu to suit your taste. If using the hemp oil, sprinkle it over the soup just before serving.

Chilled Asparagus Soup ....

5 to 6 cups Almond Milk (page 34) or Cashew Milk (page 40)

2 pounds asparagus, trimmed and sliced

1½ cups sliced leeks

1 tablespoon chopped fresh tarragon

1 tablespoon chopped fresh chervil

1 teaspoon Celtic sea salt

¼ teaspoon ground cinnamon

Dash of turmeric

3 to 4 teaspoons raw hemp oil or olive oil (optional)

Combine the milk, asparagus, leeks, tarragon, chervil, salt, cinnamon, and turmeric in a high-powered blender, and process until smooth. Adjust the seasonings, if necessary. Chill thoroughly. If using the hemp oil, sprinkle it over the soup just before serving.

Chilled Watercress and Pear Soup

YIELD: 5 TO 6 SERVINGS

4 pears, cored and diced

2 ounces (85 grams) watercress, plus additional for garnish

1 cup Almond Milk (page 34) or Cashew Milk (page 40)

1 onion, coarsely chopped

1 cup celery juice

1 tablespoon raw olive oil or grapeseed oil

Celtic sea salt, to taste

Ground cardamom, to taste

Combine all the ingredients in a high-powered blender, and process on high until smooth. Adjust the seasonings to taste, if necessary. Chill thoroughly before serving. Garnish with a few sprigs of watercress.

Curried Parsnip Soup .... YIELD: 5 TO 6 SERVINGS

This soup makes a warming addition to an autumn or winter holiday meal.

2 cups Cashew Milk (page 40) or Almond Milk (page 34)

2 cups celery juice

4 parsnips, sliced (peeling is optional)

1 small onion, quartered

2 to 4 teaspoons freshly squeezed lemon juice

2 teaspoons mild or medium-hot curry paste or curry powder

1 teaspoon ground cumin

1 teaspoon ground coriander

1 garlic clove

½ teaspoon ground cinnamon

Chives, sliced, for garnish

Combine the milk, celery juice, parsnips, onion, lemon juice, curry paste, cumin, coriander, garlic, and cinnamon in a high-powered blender, and process until the desired texture is achieved. Adjust the seasonings to taste. Ladle into individual soup bowls, and garnish with chives.

E₃Live Salsa

E3Live Salsa

YIELD: 5 TO 6 SERVINGS

5 large, ripe tomatoes, chopped

3 tablespoons freshly squeezed lime juice

3 tablespoons minced fresh cilantro

1 to 2 jalapeño chiles, seeded and minced

1 ripe avocado, finely diced

1 small onion, finely chopped

1 tablespoon E3Live, or 2 to 4 capsules E3AFA, or 1 to 2 teaspoons E3AFA crystal flakes (see page 13)

2 garlic cloves, minced

1 teaspoon Himalayan salt

Combine all the ingredients in a bowl and mix well.

Fruity Avocado Soup

YIELD: 4 SERVINGS

2 ripe avocados

2 cups water, more or less as needed

1 cup chopped pineapple

2 bananas

Combine all the ingredients in a high-powered blender, and process until the desired texture is achieved. Adjust the amount of water as needed. Serve thoroughly chilled.

Avocado Salsa

YIELD: 5 TO 6 SERVINGS

1 very ripe avocado

1 tablespoon freshly squeezed lemon juice

1 cucumber, diced

½ red chile, seeded and finely chopped

Peel and dice the avocado. Transfer to a bowl, and toss it with the lemon juice to prevent it from turning brown (or simply cut the avocado with a ceramic knife). Add the cucumber and chile, and toss again gently.

Gazpacho with Avocado Salsa

2¼ pounds tomatoes

2½ cups chilled water

1 cucumber, chopped

1 red bell pepper, chopped

1 lemon, juiced

1 lime, juiced

2 tablespoons raw olive oil

2 garlic cloves, chopped

1 red chile, seeded and chopped

2 drops Sambal Olek (page 154)

Celtic sea salt

Cayenne

Avocado Salsa (page 89)

1 handful fresh basil, for garnish

Combine the tomatoes, water, cucumber, bell pepper, lemon juice, lime juice, olive oil, garlic, chile, and Sambal Olek in a high-powered blender or food processor fitted with the S blade. Process just until blended but still chunky. Season with salt and cayenne to taste. Chill thoroughly. Make the Avocado Salsa just before serving. Top each bowl of soup with some of the salsa, and garnish with the basil.

Green Energy Soup ....

YIELD: 2 TO 3 SERVINGS

2 apples, peeled and chopped

1 handful sunflower sprouts

½ cup green pea sprouts

1 ripe avocado

¼ cup raw dulse, soaked

Celtic sea salt

Cayenne

1 to 2 zucchinis, shredded

10 cherry tomatoes, chopped

Combine the apples, sprouts, avocado, and dulse in a high-powered blender, and process until smooth. Season with salt and cayenne to taste. Add the zucchinis and tomatoes. Stir with a ladle, and serve.

Green Soup

1 collard leaf

1 kale leaf

1 to 2 garlic cloves

2 celery stalks

1 large tomato

¼ cup freshly squeezed lemon juice, more or less to taste

½ teaspoon Nama Shoyu

¼ teaspoon cayenne, or ¼ jalapeño chile, seeded and chopped

1 to 2 green onions, chopped

Roll the garlic in the kale leaf and collard leaf and push through the hopper of a juicer with the celery. Pour into a high-powered blender. Add the tomato and lemon juice, and process until smooth. Add the Nama Shoyu and cayenne. Blend briefly, and adjust the seasonings to taste. Pour into soup bowls, and garnish with the chopped green onions.

VARIATION—QUICK GREEN SOUP: For a thicker and quicker version, combine all the ingredients, except the green onions, in a high-powered blender. Add a little water, and process until smooth. Garnish with the green onions.

Mushroom Soup

2 cups mushrooms (button, cremini, shiitake, or a combination)

1 cup Almond Milk (page 34) or Cashew Milk (page 40)

1 handful fresh parsley

1 tablespoon raw truffle oil or hemp oil

1 teaspoon seeded and chopped red jalapeño chile

Dash of ground cinnamon or nutmeg

Dash of paprika

Combine all the ingredients in a high-powered blender and pulse to obtain a thick texture. For a warm soup, process for 1 to 2 minutes and transfer to a soup tureen. Place in a dehydrator at 106 to 108 degrees F until warm. Serve immediately.

Miso Soup ....

5 cups hot water

1 daikon, grated

1 carrot, grated

½ cup minced green onions

¼ cup sliced raw dulse

¼ cup chopped raw wakame

3 tablespoons unpasteurized raw miso (preferably not from soy)

1 teaspoon Japanese sea salt

¾ teaspoon cayenne

¼ teaspoon grated orange peel, or ½ cup freshly squeezed orange juice

Combine all the ingredients in a heat-proof bowl, and place in a dehydrator at 108 degrees F for 1 to 2 hours. Adjust the miso and salt to your taste, and serve.

VARIATION—QUICK MISO SOUP: Combine the hot water, dulse, wakame, miso, salt, and cayenne in a high-powered blender. Process on high speed for about 3 minutes, then at medium speed for another 2 to 3 minutes longer. Add the daikon and carrot and pulse for about 30 seconds. Adjust the miso and salt seasonings to taste, if necessary. Pour into soup bowls, and garnish with the green onions.

Shiitake Mushroom Seaweed Soup

6 shiitake mushrooms, thoroughly cleaned

4 medium pieces raw wakame

6 cups warm water

2 tablespoons dehydrated vegetable stock powder (optional)

2 cups coconut water and flesh

1 onion, quartered and thinly sliced

2 tablespoons minced fresh ginger

3 garlic cloves, chopped

2 tablespoons chopped raw dulse

2 to 3 tablespoons Nama Shoyu

1 tablespoon umeboshi vinegar

Celtic sea salt

Cayenne

3 tablespoons minced green onions

Edible flowers (optional)

Clean the mushrooms and rinse the wakame. Soak them in two cups of the warm water with the dehydrated vegetable stock powder for about 15 minutes or until soft. Drain and reserve the liquid.

Place the soak liquid, coconut flesh, onion, ginger, and garlic in a high-powered blender, and process on medium speed until smooth. Cut off the stems of the mushrooms and discard them. Thinly slice the mushrooms and chop the wakame. Add the mushrooms and wakame to a soup tureen or bowl. Add the remaining 4 cups warm water, the blended mixture, and the dulse. Season with the Nama Shoyu, vinegar, and salt and cayenne to taste. Add the green onions and optional edible flowers, and chill thoroughly before serving.

NOTE: For a warm soup during winter, place it in a dehydrator at 108 degrees F for 2 to 4 hours. Garnish with the green onions and optional edible flowers just before serving.

Thick and Spicy Minestrone Soup

This soup is the perfect choice for a cold winter meal when you are tempted to return to cooked foods. It is very filling and nutrient dense.

5 cups chopped celery

3 to 4 cups chopped Granny Smith apples

2 cups raw corn kernels (optional)

2 cups sprouted lentils

1 cup sprouted green peas (optional)

1 cup sprouted chickpeas

2 red bell peppers, chopped

1 yellow squash, cubed

1 sweet yam, cubed

6 to 8 tomatoes, chopped (use only if in season)

4 to 7 cups water

2 cups carrot juice or vegetable broth

3 cups chopped onions

1 cup finely chopped fresh basil

½ cup finely chopped fresh tarragon

3 to 5 tablespoons freshly squeezed lemon juice

3 to 5 tablespoons Nama Shoyu

4 tablespoons ground cumin

2 to 3 tablespoons Celtic sea salt

2 tablespoons finely chopped fresh rosemary

1 piece (2 to 4 inches long) fresh ginger, or 2 teaspoons ground ginger

1 tablespoon turmeric

1 to 2 teaspoons cayenne or crushed red chile flakes

1 teaspoon saffron

2 to 3 garlic cloves

2 to 3 cups finely chopped fresh parsley

2 cups finely chopped fresh cilantro

Place the celery, apples, corn, sprouts, bell peppers, squash, and yam in large soup tureen or bowl. Add the tomatoes, water, carrot juice, garlic, 1 1/2 cups of the onions, 1/2 cup of the basil, and 1/4 cup of the tarragon. Stir in the lemon juice, Nama Shoyu, cumin, salt, rosemary, ginger, turmeric, cayenne, saffron, and garlic in a high-powered blender, and process until smooth. Pour into the soup tureen and add all the remaining ingredients. Stir well, and let rest for 4 to 12 hours (at room temperature or in the refrigerator, depending on the climate) to allow the flavors to blend (the longer it rests, the better it tastes). Serve at room temperature.

NOTES: For additional warming energy, add 1 to 2 cups additional water and place the soup in a dehydrator at 106 to 108 degrees F for 3 to 5 hours before serving.

• If fresh tomatoes are not in season, use 10 to 12 dried tomatoes soaked for 2 to 3 hours instead.

Spicy Minestrone Soup .... YIELD: 12 SERVINGS

8 to 10 cups water

2 to 3 leeks, finely chopped

1 to 2 lemons or limes, juiced

2 to 4 tablespoons Nama Shoyu

2 to 3 garlic cloves

8 to 10 tomatoes, chopped (use heirloom tomatoes, if available)

1 handful mixed fresh herbs (such as marjoram, thyme, and oregano)

4 cups sprouted lentils

4 to 6 zucchinis, finely chopped

2 cups bite-size cauliflower florets

2 cups bite-size broccoli florets

1 cup raw cashews

1 red jalapeño chile, seeded and finely chopped

1 to 2 ripe avocados, diced

½ teaspoon cayenne

Dash of cardamom

Place the water, leeks, lemon juice, Nama Shoyu, and garlic in a high-powered blender, and process on high until very smooth. Add the tomatoes and the herbs, and process again on high speed. Transfer to a soup tureen and add the sprouts, zucchinis, cauliflower, broccoli, cashews, and chile. Mix well. Chill in the refrigerator for 2 to 4 hours before serving to allow the flavors to blend. Add the avocado and cardamom just before serving.

NOTE: For a warm soup during winter, place in a dehydrator at 105 degrees F for at least 4 hours. Add the avocado and cardamom just before serving.

Chicory and Bean Soup

YIELD: 6 TO 7 SERVINGS

This makes a hearty main dish.

6 to 8 cups water

4 to 5 cups chopped chicory

2 cups sprouted beans

4 to 6 tablespoons Nama Shoyu

2 vegetable bouillon cubes

2 onions, minced

5 to 6 celery stalks, chopped

4 to 5 zucchinis, cubed

4 carrots, chopped

6 cherry tomatoes, whole

1 tablespoon turmeric

2 garlic cloves, minced

1 teaspoon cayenne

1 teaspoon raw dulse flakes

Dash of chili powder

1 cup raw olive oil

6 cherry tomatoes, chopped

Combine the water, chicory, sprouted beans, Nama Shoyu, and bouillon cubes in a high-powered blender, and pulse 3 or 4 times. Add the onions, celery, zucchinis, carrots, whole cherry tomatoes, turmeric, garlic, cayenne, dulse, and chili powder, and pulse a few more times. Blend on low speed for 1 minutes, drizzling in the oil through the cap opening. Ladle into soup bowls. Garnish with the chopped cherry tomatoes.

Appetizers

These tasty nibbles may be served as hors d'oeuvres, to whet the appetite for a larger meal to follow, or they can be enjoyed as snacks. In larger portions or in combination with other recipes in this book, they can be used as part of a complete meal. These are sure to impress your guests at parties and festive gatherings, especially those who are new to raw vegan cuisine.

Stuffed Cherry Tomatoes ....

12 firm cherry tomatoes, stems removed

1 to 2 tablespoons Herb Butter (page 155)

Curly parsley, for garnish

¼ teaspoon asafoetida

Using a sharp knife point, loosen the insides of each tomato (or use a tomato scooper). Scoop out the seeds and juices, leaving only the tomato shells. Take care to not puncture holes in the sides. Stuff with the Herb Butter. Arrange on a white plate, garnish with parsley, and sprinkle with the asafoetida.

Creamy Mushrooms .... Yield: 3 to 4 servings

2 portobello mushrooms, stems removed and thoroughly cleaned

1 cup button mushrooms, stems removed and thoroughly cleaned

½ ripe avocado

½ onion, chopped

1 lemon, juiced

1 garlic clove

¼ teaspoon asafoetida

Chop the portobello mushrooms, and place them in a serving dish. Combine the remaining ingredients in a high-powered blender, and process until smooth. Pour over the portobello mushrooms and serve.

NOTE: This dish may also be used as a sauce for Raw Spaghetti (page 138) and served as a meal.

Eggplant and Walnut Tomato Cups

1 eggplant, cut into 1-inch chunks (peel if the skin is too bitter)

1 onion, chopped

1 red bell pepper, chopped

¼ cup raw apple cider vinegar

2 tablespoons chopped fresh basil

1 jalapeño chile, seeded (optional)

2 tablespoons chopped raw walnuts

1 tablespoon raw capers

1 teaspoon Celtic sea salt

Dash of freshly squeezed lemon juice

1 pound large cherry tomatoes

Raw mustard oil (optional)

Place the eggplant, onion, bell pepper, vinegar, basil, and chile in a food processor fitted with the S blade, and processor until coarsely chopped. Add the walnuts and capers, and process until thick and coarsely blended. Season with the salt and lemon juice to taste.

Using a sharp knife point, loosen the insides of each tomato (or use a tomato scooper). Scoop out and reserve the seeds and juices, leaving only the tomato shells. Take care to not puncture holes in the sides. Add the seeds and tomato juices to the mixture in the food processor, and process until well incorporated. Using a small spoon, fill each tomato with the walnut mixture, or use a pastry bag. Place the stuffed tomatoes in a dish, sprinkle with mustard oil, if desired, and serve. Alternatively, place in a dehydrator at 105 to 108 degrees F until the desired texture is achieved.

NOTE: Instead of using a pastry bag to stuff the tomatoes, place the walnut mixture in a zipper-lock plastic bag. Seal the bag, and make a small diagonal cut on one of the lower corners. Press the mixture through the cut.

Fig Fiesta ....

This very simple recipe is a perennial raw party favorite, as are the variations on this page and the next.

4 ripe figs

6 to 8 raspberries

Spearmint leaves, for garnish (optional)

Stand the figs vertically so they are resting on the thick, flat portion of the bottom of the fruit. Carefully cut off the stem along with a small portion of the top of the fig, creating a cap that will cover the fig later. Scoop out the insides very carefully, so as not to pierce the skin of the fruit. Place the scooped out portion in a bowl. Add the raspberries to the bowl and mash them together with a fork, blending well. Stuff this mixture back inside the fig with a small spoon or funnel, and cover with the reserved cap. Serve on a white plate or platter, and drizzle the with any syrup that remains from the mashed fruit mixture. Garnish with spearmint leaves, if desired.

Minty Fig Fiesta ....

4 ripe figs

3 to 4 raspberries

2 stalks fresh peppermint leaves, minced

Peppermint leaves, for garnish

Stand the figs vertically so they are resting on the thick, flat portion of the bottom of the fruit. Carefully cut off the stem along with a small portion of the top of the fig, creating a cap that will cover the fig later. Scoop out the insides very carefully, so as not to pierce the skin of the fruit. Place the scooped out portion in a bowl. Add the raspberries and minced peppermint to the bowl and mash them together with a fork, blending well. Stuff this mixture back inside the fig with a small spoon or funnel. Insert a whole peppermint leaf on one side of the filling, and place the reserved cap on the stuffed fig so the peppermint leaf is coming out from underneath it. Scatter whole peppermint leaves around the serving plate.

Chlorophyll Fig Fiesta.............. YIELD: 2 SERVINGS

4 ripe figs

2 to 4 fresh strawberries

2 stalks fresh peppermint, minced

1 teaspoon E3Live, defrosted

Peppermint leaves, for garnish (optional)

Stand the figs vertically so they are resting on the thick, flat portion of the bottom of the fruit. Carefully cut off the stem along with a small portion of the top of the fig, creating a cap that will cover the fig later. Scoop out the insides very carefully, so as not to pierce the skin of the fruit. Place the scooped out portion in a bowl. Add the strawberries, E3Live, and minced peppermint to the bowl, and mash them together with a fork, blending well. Stuff this mixture back inside the fig with a small spoon or funnel, and cover with the reserved cap. Insert a whole peppermint leaf on one side of the filling, and place the reserved cap on the stuffed fig so the peppermint leaf is coming out from underneath it. Scatter whole peppermint leaves around the serving plate.

Fig-Banana Delight .... YIELD: 3 SERVINGS

This recipe is loaded with fiber, which is often lacking in the modern diet. It makes a refreshing and filling appetizer.

6 to 8 ripe figs

1 to 2 very ripe bananas

1 teaspoon unsweetened shredded dried coconut

Stand the figs vertically so they are resting on the thick, flat portion of the bottom of the fruit. Carefully cut off the stem along with a small portion of the top of the fig. Scoop out the insides very carefully, so as not to pierce the skin of the fruit. Place the scooped out portion in a bowl, add the bananas, and mash them together with a fork. Stuff this mixture back inside the fig with a small spoon or funnel, and sprinkle with the coconut. Chill thoroughly before serving.

Custardy Durian Spread ...... YIELD: 6 TO 7 SERVINGS

Enjoy by candlelight!

1 cup ripe durian
4 celery stalks, cut in half

Mash the durian, and spread it on the celery stalks.

NOTE: Because Durian has a very strong and pungent smell, if you will be serving this to guests, be sure to warn them about the aroma beforehand.

Grape Salad .... YIELD: 3 TO 4 SERVINGS

3 ounces green grapes, cut in half
3 ounces black grapes, cut in half
2 Red Delicious apples, finely chopped
1 tablespoon raisins
1 teaspoon freshly squeezed lemon juice
Coconut Frosting (page 181; optional)

Combine the grapes, apples, raisins, and lemon juice in a bowl. Mix well. Top with Coconut Frosting, if desired, and serve.

Pear Bear Blankets ....

This is a great winter holiday project for children, and a wonderful hors d'oeuvre to serve to guests, which the children can serve themselves to show what they made. Use it as a show-and-tell game to include their participation at holiday gatherings.

1 medium pear, cored and cut into 8 wedges

¼ teaspoon freshly squeezed lemon juice

8 thin slices zucchini

2 tablespoons Cranberry Pear Sauce (page 176)

Dip the pear wedges in the lemon juice, and put on a plate Spread each slice of zucchini with the Cranberry Pear Sauce. Wrap the zucchini around each pear wedge and secure with a toothpick. Arrange on a serving plate.

NOTE: Use a mandoline to slice long strips of the zucchini. Do not let children anywhere near the mandoline, and certainly do not let them slice with it unless you are completely confident with their level of expertise and attention to safety.

Quick Kimchee ....

Serve Kimchee by itself as an appetizer or with Germinated Brown Rice (page 131) as a meal.

5 heads cabbage

3 ½ pounds rock salt

10 chestnuts

2 radishes

5 heads garlic

½ bunch large green onions

3 grams ginger roots

1 bunch Japanese parsley

½ bunch small green onions

½ bunch mustard leaves

2 pears

5 manna lichen mushrooms, soaked

5 shiitake mushrooms, soaked

2 teaspoons shredded red chiles

10 pitted dates

½ cup Himalayan salt

Dash of agave nectar

Cut the cabbages either in half or in quarters, and soak in water to which the rock salt has been added, for about 5 hours.

Shred the chestnuts, radishes, and garlic, and slice the large green onions. Cut the Japanese parsley, small green onions, and mustard leaves into 1 ½-inch-long pieces. Shred 1 pear and cut the other pear into quarters.

Drain and shred the manna lichen mushrooms and shiitake mushrooms. Cut the shredded chiles into 1-inch pieces, and mince the shredded garlic.

Drain the cabbage (reserve the soak water) and place it and the shredded radish in a bowl. Add the shredded red chile. Season with some of Himalayan salt and add the shredded chestnuts, large green onions, parsley, mustard leaves, pears, manna lichen mushrooms, shiitake mushrooms, and whole dates.

Add the small green onions, garlic, and ginger roots, and mix well. Add the agave nectar and the remaining salt to taste. Spread the cabbage soak water over the cabbage. Store in an airtight jar in the refrigerator until you are ready to use it.

Guacamole .... YIELD: 4 TO 5 SERVINGS

2 ripe avocados, finely diced

1 cup chopped tomatoes

½ cup chopped fresh cilantro

1 small onion, finely chopped

½ lemon, juiced

1 jalapeño chile, seeded and finely chopped

1 garlic clove, minced

½ teaspoon Celtic sea salt

¼ teaspoon asafoetida

Combine all the ingredients in a bowl. Adjust the seasonings to taste.

NOTE: This recipe may be served as a dip or on raw crackers, breads, or crudités. It may also be used in the recipes in this book for wraps or burritos, or used as a filling for Savory Pie Crust (page 193).

Ground Avocado .... YIELD: 3 TO 4 SERVINGS

Let the children in your life make this, and give them an opportunity to have fun with a mortar and pestle while preparing something the entire family will enjoy.

2 garlic cloves

¼ teaspoon Himalayan salt

Dash of ground serrano chile

2 ripe avocados

6 tomatillos

1 yellow or white onion, sliced (optional)

2 tablespoons chopped fresh cilantro

Grind the garlic in a mortar using a pestle. Add the salt and chile and grind again. Add the avocados and tomatillos and grind a little more. Garnish with onions slices, if desired, and top with the cilantro. Serve immediately.

Herbed Mushrooms ....

These are a huge party favorite.

12 to 24 button or cremini mushrooms, stems removed

2 cups Herb Butter (page 155)

3 to 6 tablespoons raw olive oil or grapeseed oil

2 to 4 teaspoon Nama Shoyu or Celtic sea salt

2 to 4 garlic cloves, minced

Dash of cayenne

Dash of asafoetida

Place the mushrooms on a baking tray. Combine the Herb Butter, oil, Nama Shoyu, garlic, cayenne, and asafoetida in a small bowl and mix well. Fill the mushroom caps with this mixture. Place the stuffed mushrooms in a dehydrator for 2 to 3 hours (depending on how moist or dry you wish them to be) and serve at once.

Holiday Chestnuts ....

Spread this mixture on celery sticks or wrap it in lettuce leaves for a very tasty hors d'oeuvre. You can also put it in a dipping dish and serve it as a butter or spread. Alternatively, try it as a dessert topping during the winter holidays.

24 chestnuts

3 tablespoons raw flaxseed oil

3 tablespoons agave nectar

1/4 teaspoon fennel seeds (optional)

Place the chestnuts in a dehydrator at 110 degrees F for about 1 hour. Crack open the skin, remove the flesh, and place it in a high-powered blender along with the remaining ingredients. Process until smooth.

Curried Jicama with Shiitake Gravy

YIELD: 6 TO 8 SERVINGS

This is a great substitute for cooked mashed potatoes and gravy.

2 to 3 jicamas, shredded

¾ cup celery juice

1 tablespoon raw flaxseed oil or olive oil

1 teaspoon curry powder, more or less to taste (optional)

½ cup raw tahini

10 shiitake mushrooms

¼ onion

1 tablespoon Nama Shoyu

1½ teaspoons Celtic sea salt

1 garlic clove

Place the shredded jicama in a food processor fitted with the S blade. Add a small amount of the celery juice (about ¼ cup, as needed), and process until it is the consistency of mashed potatoes. Add a small amount of the oil, making sure the consistency remains thick like mashed potatoes. Add the optional curry powder, and set aside

To make the gravy, combine the remaining celery juice and the tahini, shiitake mushrooms, onion, Nama Shoyu, and garlic in a high-powered blender. Process until smooth and creamy. Spoon a small amount of this gravy over the jicama and serve.

Mushroom Walnut Hors D'oeuvres

YIELD: 5 TO 7 SERVINGS

12 to 24 large button mushrooms

2 cups chopped spinach

1 cup finely chopped onions

2 tablespoons raw pine nuts, chopped

2 tablespoons finely chopped parsley

1 tablespoon chopped raw walnuts

1 garlic clove, finely chopped

½ teaspoon raw olive oil, plus additional as needed

¼ teaspoon Celtic sea salt

¼ teaspoon cayenne

Dash of ground nutmeg

Edible flowers, for garnish (optional)

Clean the mushrooms thoroughly with a dry cloth and remove the stems. Set the caps aside, and place the stems in a food processor fitted with the S blade. Add the remaining the ingredients to the food processor, and process until everything is finely chopped. Stuff the mushroom caps with this mixture, and place them in a shallow dish. Sprinkle with a little extra olive oil and place in a dehydrator at 105 degrees F for 1 to 2 hours. Garnish with edible flowers, if desired. Serve at once.

Nutty Brussels Sprouts ....

1 pound Brussels sprouts

1 tablespoon raw mustard oil or olive oil

Dash of Flower of the Ocean sea minerals

8 to 12 raw hazelnuts or almonds, soaked

1 teaspoon ground cardamom

Dash of ground nutmeg

Dash of asafoetida

Crushed raw hazelnuts

Wash the Brussels sprouts, cut off the stems, and remove any loose leaves. Cut the Brussels sprouts in half, place them in a medium bowl, and add the oil and sea minerals. Let marinate for 8 to 12 hours (at room temperature or in the refrigerator, depending on the climate).

Combine the soaked hazelnuts, cardamom, nutmeg, asafoetida, and a small amount of water in a high-powered blender Process until smooth, and pour over the Brussels sprouts. Add a few extra crushed hazelnuts and sea minerals to taste.

Olive Pâté ....

Serve this delicious spread with celery and cucumber sticks, or spread it on Buckwheat Crackers (page 24) for a raw pizza.

1 cup pitted raw olives

1 large onion, finely chopped

¼ cup seedless dark raisins

2 tablespoons blended tomatoes

1½ teaspoons finely minced fresh oregano

1 teaspoon ground cumin

2 garlic cloves, finely chopped

¼ teaspoon Celtic sea salt (optional)

Dash of asafoetida

Combine all the ingredients in a high-powered blender or a food processor fitted with the S blade. Adjust the seasonings to taste.

Tomatillos..............................

Serve this with slices of ripe avocado or lettuce leaves.

¼ cup raw apple cider vinegar

2 finely minced shallots

¾ cup raw olive oil

3 to 4 tomatillos, finely chopped

½ cup chopped fresh basil

2 tablespoons chopped fresh oregano

2 tablespoons chopped fresh marjoram

½ teaspoon Celtic sea salt

1 serrano chile, seeded and chopped

Dash of cayenne

Whisk together the vinegar and shallots. Slowly add the oil, whisking constantly. Stir in the remaining ingredients, and whisk until everything is well blended.

Southern-Style Corn ....

Yield: 6 cups

2½ cups raw corn kernels

3 celery stalks, chopped

1 cup diced red bell peppers

1 cup pitted raw olives, diced

½ cup diced poblano chiles

½ cup diced red onions

3 stalks cilantro, chopped

1½ teaspoons freshly squeezed lime juice

1 tablespoon raw mustard oil, olive oil, or hemp oil

1½ teaspoons Flower of the Ocean sea minerals or Himalayan salt

½ teaspoon ground cumin

¼ teaspoon fennel seeds (optional)

Combine all the ingredients in a large bowl. Adjust the seasonings to taste, and serve.

Spicy Avocado Salad ....

1 ripe avocado, cubed

1 cup diced tomatoes

1 ear of corn, kernels removed

½ cup chopped fresh cilantro

1 to 2 limes, juiced

2 tablespoons chopped raw olives

1 tablespoon chopped green onions

1 tablespoon chopped jalapeño chile, or less to taste

1 small garlic clove, minced

Dash of Celtic sea salt

Dash of asafoetida

Gently combine all the ingredients in a bowl. Adjust the lime juice, salt, and jalapeño chile to taste.

Tomatoes and Red Peppers ....

4 pounds heirloom tomatoes (various colors)

2 pounds red bell peppers

½ cup raw olive oil

3 tablespoons crushed garlic

4 leaves fresh basil, finely chopped

3 dried chiles

1 tablespoon sweet paprika

½ teaspoon Celtic sea salt

¼ teaspoon Atlantic kelp powder

Edible flowers, for garnish

Chop the tomatoes and bell peppers into large pieces, and transfer to a serving platter or bowl. Save the juice running out of the tomatoes, and put it in a high-powered blender along with the olive oil, garlic, basil, dried chiles, paprika, salt, and kelp. Pulse several times. Pour over the tomatoes and bell peppers. Serve at room temperature or thoroughly chilled. Garnish with edible flowers.

Tricolor Salad ....

This is a very quick and satisfying dish.

4 large plum tomatoes, sliced

2 jicamas, sliced

1 large, ripe avocado

1 bunch fresh basil

3 tablespoons raw olive oil

Dash of Celtic sea salt

Dash of herbes de Provence

Dash of cayenne

Dash of Atlantic kelp granules

1 spearmint sprig

Arrange the sliced tomatoes and jicama on two plates. Sprinkle with a dash of the salt (this will draw out some of the juices from the tomatoes). Set aside in the refrigerator, and let marinate for about 30 minutes.

Just before serving, cut the avocado in half. Remove the pit, and slice it crosswise into half-moons (remove the peel). Arrange it over the tomatoes and jicama. Mince some of the basil leaves and sprinkle them on top. Whisk together the olive oil, salt, herbes de Provence, and cayenne, and drizzle over the plate of salad. Sprinkle with a dash of kelp, and garnish with the spearmint and remaining basil.

Wild Mushroom Pâté .... YIELD: 5 TO 6 SERVINGS

This is a huge favorite at parties, so make extra if you want it to last a while.

10 ounces mixed porcini and cremini wild mushrooms, chopped

½ cup minced shallots

6 to 8 pitted raw olives

3 tablespoons raw pine nuts

2 tablespoons finely chopped parsley

2 garlic cloves, minced

1 tablespoon freshly squeezed lemon juice

1 tablespoon raw olive oil or truffle oil

2 teaspoons minced fresh marjoram

1 teaspoon Nama Shoyu

1 teaspoon grated lemon peel

½ teaspoon cayenne

Dash of paprika

Parsley sprigs

8 to 10 cucumbers, sliced

Place the mushrooms, shallots, olives, pine nuts, chopped parsley, garlic, lemon juice, oil, marjoram, Nama Shoyu, lemon peel, and cayenne in a food processor fitted with the S blade. Process into a smooth paste. Add more Nama Shoyu, if needed. Transfer to a serving platter, and garnish with a dash of paprika and parsley sprigs. Arrange the sliced cucumbers around the edge of the platter. Alternatively, spread the pâté on the cucumber slices and serve as hors d'oeuvres.

*M*ain *D*ishes

Although almost all the recipes in this book can be served as a meal, this section emphasizes dishes that are, for the most part, heavier and more filling. No matter what your preferences may be, you are certain to find something in this section that not only appeals to you but also to your family and friends. These recipes allow you to have fabulous dinner parties, brunches, and celebrations, just as you did when you ate cooked food, without being concerned that your guests won't be satisfied.

Note: If you are not used to eating sea vegetables on a regular basis, start out with recipes that call for arame, nori, or dulse, as these are the most mild tasting ones.

Asparagus with Cashews .... Yield: 6 servings

1½ pounds asparagus

2 tablespoons raw olive oil

1 tablespoon finely chopped fresh ginger

2 teaspoons raw sesame oil

½ cup coarsely chopped raw cashews

1 tablespoon Nama Shoyu

1 tablespoon freshly squeezed orange juice

1 teaspoon kelp granules

Trim off the tough lower stem of the asparagus and reserve it for juicing. Cut each stalk diagonally into 2 or 3 pieces. Place the pieces in a medium bowl. Add the olive oil, ginger, and sesame oil, and marinate for 8 to 12 hours (at room temperature or in the refrigerator, depending on the climate).

About 1 to 2 hours before serving, stir in the cashews, Nama Shoyu, and orange juice. Sprinkle with the kelp just before serving.

Cheezy Tortilla Rolls .... Yield: 6 to 8 rolls

This makes a great tortilla for a wrap using Guacamole (page 106), Ground Avocado (page 106), and Spicy Salsa (page 161).

3 cups raw corn kernels

½ cup chopped fresh cilantro

½ cup freshly squeezed orange juice

½ cup flaxseeds, soaked

1 tablespoon Celtic sea salt

1 teaspoon ground cumin

1 teaspoon chopped habanero chile

1 teaspoon minced fresh ginger

1 teaspoon minced garlic (optional)

1 teaspoon freshly squeezed lime juice and pulp

Place all the ingredients in a food processor fitted with the S blade, and process until well combined. Spoon onto unbleached waxed paper or parchment paper, and form into ¼-inch-thick circles, 3 to 6 inches in diameter. Dehydrate at 115 degrees F for about 5 hours, or until the texture is chewy (do not dry completely, unless you want to make cheezy chips).

NOTE: Instead of circles, you can cut the mixture into strips.

Asian Mung Bean Salad ......

This dish will satisfy the cravings of those who love the flavor of cooked Chinese food.

2 cups mung bean sprouts

2 cups snow peas

2 cups chopped bok choy

1 cup sunflower sprouts

1 cup chopped napa cabbage

1 cup thinly sliced shiitake mushrooms (optional)

1 cup finely chopped fresh cilantro

3 tablespoons freshly squeezed orange juice (optional)

2 to 3 tablespoons Nama Shoyu

2 to 4 tablespoons raw sesame oil

2 tablespoons umeboshi vinegar

1 to 2 tablespoons agave nectar (optional)

1 tablespoon Chinese five-spice powder

1 teaspoon Celtic sea salt

2 garlic cloves

1 slice fresh ginger

Combine the mung bean sprouts, snow peas, bok choy, sunflower sprouts, cabbage, and optional mushrooms in a large bowl. Place the cilantro, orange juice, Nama Shoyu, sesame oil, vinegar, agave nectar, Chinese five-spice powder, salt, garlic, and ginger in a high-powered blender, and process until smooth and well blended. Ad just the seasonings to taste. Pour over the vegetables and marinate for 2 to 3 hours (at room temperature or in the refrigerator, depending on the climate) before serving, stirring occasionally.

Arame Mushroom Cups .... YIELD: 6 SERVINGS

For a simple dish with a lot of taste, try this one.

1 cup raw arame

18 large mushrooms

1 medium onion, coarsely chopped

¼ cup yacon syrup or agave nectar

1 lemon, juiced

2 tablespoons Nama Shoyu

1 tablespoon peeled and chopped fresh ginger

1 teaspoon raw sesame oil

2 to 3 lemon slices, for garnish

1 teaspoon minced fresh parsley, for garnish

Soak the arame for about 10 minutes. Rinse well and drain. Rinse the mushrooms and remove the stems. Place the mushroom caps on a large serving dish. Dice the mushroom stems, and set them aside in a large mixing bowl. Mince the arame and add it to the bowl with the mushroom stems. Combine the onion, yacon syrup, lemon juice, Nama Shoyu, and ginger in a high-powered blender, and process until smooth

Pour half of the blended mixture over the arame and mushroom stems and stir well. Stuff the mushroom caps with the arame mixture. Pour the remaining blended mixture over the mushroom caps and sprinkle the oil on top. Place the dish with the mushrooms in a dehydrator at 105 degrees F for 30 to 35 minutes. Garnish with the lemon slices and parsley just before serving.

Asian Spring Rolls ....

This is a very popular dish at dinner parties.

4 to 6 sheets raw rice paper (one for each spring roll; see notes)

3 cups chopped napa cabbage

1 cup bean sprouts

2 to 4 shiitake mushrooms, thinly sliced

⅓ cup dry white wine or grape juice

2 to 3 tablespoons Nama Shoyu

½ cup chopped sweet onions

¼ teaspoon Chinese five-spice powder

1 teaspoon minced garlic

1 teaspoon minced fresh ginger

1 teaspoon raw sesame oil

1½ teaspoons raw black sesame seeds, soaked (see notes)

Raw Mustard (page 160)

Place the rice paper on a bamboo mat for rolling, and set aside.

Put the cabbage, bean sprouts and mushrooms in a medium bowl. Place the wine, Nama Shoyu, onions, Chinese five-spice powder, garlic, and ginger in a high-powered blender, and process until smooth. Drizzle in the oil a little at a time, and mix again. Pour half of this mixture over the vegetables and marinate for 1 to 2 hours (at room temperature or in the refrigerator, depending on the climate).

Drain the vegetables completely. Using one rice paper sheet at a time, place a portion of the vegetables on the rice paper, and roll up very tightly. Arrange the whole rolls on a platter. Sprinkle with the sesame seeds just before serving. Use the remaining marinade as a dipping sauce. Serve with Raw Mustard on the side.

NOTES • Soak the sesame seeds in a little Nama Shoyu prior to using. This will imitate the flavor of traditional Asian dishes.

• If raw rice paper is not available, roll the vegetables in cabbage leaves or raw nori sheets instead.

Spicy Black Beans ....

This dish is for those who love hot, spicy dishes. Serve it by itself or with Germinated Brown Rice (page 131).

3 cups sprouted black beans

2 to 3 zucchinis, cut into bite-size pieces

½ cup chopped onions

6 to 8 cherry tomatoes, quartered

3 to 4 tablespoons freshly squeezed lime juice

3 garlic cloves, minced

1 jalapeño chile, seeded and minced

1 teaspoon raw mustard oil or chili oil

1 teaspoon Celtic sea salt

1 teaspoon raw dulse flakes

Combine all the ingredients in a serving bowl, and mix thoroughly. Refrigerate for a few hours. Serve at room temperature or thoroughly chilled.

Sweet-and-Spicy Brown Rice ....

1 cup Germinated Brown Rice (see note)

3 cups water

½ cup raisins

3 garlic cloves, chopped

1 teaspoon raw olive oil

1 teaspoon cayenne

1 teaspoon Celtic sea salt

1 teaspoon dried parsley flakes

1 teaspoon dried basil

Soak the rice in the water for 4 to 12 hours (the longer you soak the rice, the softer it will be). Drain and add all the remaining ingredients. Mix well. Serve at room temperature.

VARIATION: Add ripe avocado chunks just before serving for an extra-special flavor.

NOTE: Germinated Brown Rice is a packaged brand-name product available from Japanese outlets. It is made from Japanese brown rice that is germinated until it just begins to sprout. This process liberates nutrients to achieve maximum nutritional value and flavor. Please see www.serenityspaces.org for additional information.

Cheezy Veggie Balls ....

2 cups raw sunflower seeds, ground

2 cups shredded carrots

3 bunches green onions, chopped

1 cup chopped zucchini or other squash

1 cup shredded beets

½ cup finely chopped onions

2 tablespoons nutritional yeast (optional)

2 tablespoons Nama Shoyu

1 to 2 tablespoons dried Italian seasoning

1 tablespoon curry powder

Combine all the ingredients in a food processor fitted with the S blade, and process into a moist dough. Form into 1-inch balls using wet hands (or coat your hands with raw olive oil). Put the balls on a dehydrator tray (do not use Teflex sheets), and dehydrate at 108 to 110 degrees F for 12 to 24 hours, turning the balls over at least once.

VARIATION: The balls may be served fresh, without being dehydrated.

NOTES: The balls will keep for a long time if dehydrated, but they will become harder.

• If desired, serve with Marinara Sauce (page 157) and "Cheese" Sauce (page 150), or Rich Curry Sauce (page 164).

Chickpea Salad I....................

1 pound chickpeas, sprouted

3 celery stalks, diced

1 very ripe tomato, chopped

⅔ cup minced green onions

3 tablespoons chopped fresh parsley

3 tablespoons freshly squeezed lemon juice

2½ teaspoons chopped fresh mint

2 tablespoons raw olive oil, more or less to taste

3 garlic cloves, pressed

1 teaspoon raw dulse flakes

Celtic sea salt

Cayenne

1 small head romaine lettuce

3 tablespoons raw pine nuts

Combine the chickpea sprouts, celery, tomato, green onions, parsley, lemon juice, mint, oil, garlic, and dulse in a medium bowl. Season to taste with the salt and cayenne. Serve on a bed of the romaine lettuce, and sprinkle with the pine nuts.

Chickpeas with Tahini-Mint Dressing

Yield: 3 to 4 servings

2 to 3 cups chickpea sprouts

3 to 4 cucumbers, cubed

2 to 3 carrots, diced

3 to 4 stalks of celery, diced

½ cup chopped fresh parsley

1 turnip, grated or finely diced

¼ cup red onions, diced

½ daikon, grated

1 stalk fresh dill, finely chopped

1 tablespoon raw coconut oil (optional)

1 teaspoon raw dulse flakes

Tahini-Mint Dressing (page 80)

Combine the chickpea sprouts, cucumbers, carrots, celery, parsley, turnip, red onions, daikon, dill, and optional coconut oil in a large bowl. Mix well. Sprinkle with the dulse flakes, and serve with Tahini-Mint Dressing.

Chickpea Salad II .... YIELD: 3 TO 4 SERVINGS

This is a good choice for a fortifying meal during the cold winter months.

2 cups chickpeas, sprouted

1 cup pitted raw olives, quartered

1 cup diced red bell peppers

1 cup chopped fresh cilantro

2 celery stalks, diced

⅓ cup sliced green onions

2 tablespoons raw apple cider vinegar

2 tablespoons raw walnut oil or
  mustard oil

1 tablespoon Sambal Olek (page 154),
  more or less to taste

Celtic sea salt

Cayenne

Combine all the ingredients, except the salt and cayenne. Toss gently, seasoning gradually with the salt and cayenne to taste.

Chili Lentils .... YIELD: 3 TO 4 SERVINGS

2 to 4 cups sprouted lentils

2 cups chopped tomatoes

1 cup finely diced celery

1 cup chopped red bell peppers

1 to 2 tablespoons raw hemp oil

1 tablespoon minced fresh tarragon

1 tablespoon raw coconut oil

½ to 1 tablespoon chili powder

½ to 1 tablespoon ground cumin

2 teaspoons minced garlic

1 teaspoon Nama Shoyu

1 teaspoon Hunza black salt or Celtic
  sea salt

Dash of ground cinnamon

Lettuce or Germinated Brown Rice
  (page 131)

Combine all the ingredients, except the lettuce or Germinated Brown Rice, in a medium bowl. Adjust the seasonings to taste. Serve on a bed of lettuce or over the rice.

Vegetable Stew ....

This meal will help you to maintain a raw diet during cold winters.

2 to 4 zucchinis, cut into bite-size pieces

1 sweet potato, chopped into small chunks or shredded

1 cup green peas, preferably sprouted

1 red bell pepper, cut into bite-size pieces

6 to 8 button mushrooms, chopped

2 cups chopped tomatoes

4 tablespoons chopped fresh cilantro

2 tablespoons chopped onion

1 to 2 teaspoons raw olive oil or hemp oil

1 teaspoon freshly squeezed lemon juice (optional)

2 garlic cloves

½ teaspoon ground cumin

½ teaspoon Himalayan salt

Dash of cayenne

Put the zucchinis, sweet potato, peas, bell pepper, and mushrooms in a large mixing bowl. Briefly pulse the tomatoes in a high-powered blender. Add the cilantro, onion, oil, garlic, optional lemon juice, cumin, salt, and cayenne to the tomato purée, and pulse until combined but still chunky. Pour into the bowl with the vegetables, and mix well. Let rest for 2 to 4 hours before serving (at room temperature or in the refrigerator, depending on the climate).

NOTE: If you prefer a more warming stew, add extra cayenne and dehydrate the stew at 105 to 108 degrees F for 1 to 2 hours. Garnish with fresh cilantro and parsley and serve.

Fast and Tasty Salad ....

1 (5-ounce) bag prewashed salad greens

3 to 4 heirloom tomatoes (various colors)

2 to 4 tablespoons Nama Shoyu

2 to 4 tablespoons raw chili oil or mustard oil

1 to 2 English or pickling cucumbers

2 cups green peas (fresh or sprouted)

1 cup raw sunflower seeds (preferably sprouted)

2 tablespoons minced fresh basil

2 tablespoons minced fresh cilantro

2 tablespoons minced fresh parsley

2 tablespoons minced fresh dill

2 to 4 tablespoons raw macadamia nut oil or olive oil

6 to 10 cherry tomatoes

Place the salad greens in a large salad bowl. Thinly slice the tomatoes and put them in a dish. Add 1 to 2 tablespoons of the Nama Shoyu and 1 to 2 tablespoons of the chili oil to the tomatoes. Slice the cucumbers, and then quarter each slice. Place the cucumbers, green pea sprouts, sunflower seeds or sprouts, and chopped herbs in the bowl with the salad greens and mix well. Add the remaining Nama Shoyu and chili oil. Mix again. Add the macadamia nut oil and sliced tomatoes. Mix and add additional Nama Shoyu, if needed. Top with the cherry tomatoes before serving.

NOTES: If you prefer, you can make this salad in advance. Omit the macadamia nut oil and cherry tomatoes, and add them just before serving.

• This salad can be made without the basil, cilantro, parsley, and dill, although you will lose a lot of flavor and nutritional value. If you don't have much time, the herbs can be washed, dried, and chopped beforehand, and added when you make the salad. However, it is always best to use herbs fresh, as soon as they are picked.

Asparagus with Asian Vinaigrette

1 pound thin asparagus

3 tablespoons raw olive oil

¼ cup umeboshi vinegar

2 tablespoons Nama Shoyu

4 teaspoons raw sesame oil

½ teaspoon agave nectar

¼ teaspoon crushed red chile flakes

¼ teaspoon Hunza black salt or Himalayan salt

1 teaspoon raw coconut oil

¼ cup raw sunflower seeds

½ head red leaf lettuce

1 tablespoons diagonally sliced green onions (green part only)

Trim the ends of the asparagus, and peel them to the tip, if thick. Slice the asparagus in a long diagonal at 2-inch intervals. Soak the asparagus 8 to 12 hours in the olive oil until it is just tender to crunchy. Drain, refresh under cold running water, then dry carefully with paper towels.

To make a vinaigrette, whisk together the umeboshi vinegar, Nama Shoyu, sesame oil, agave nectar, red chile flakes, and salt. Toss with the asparagus. Cover and refrigerate for several hours before serving.

Mix the coconut oil with the sunflower seeds in a small bowl, and reserve until serving time.

When you are ready to serve the meal, toss the asparagus and vinaigrette again. Arrange a bed of lettuce leaves on individual salad plates, spoon the asparagus over the leaves, and top with the sunflower seeds and green onions.

Seaweed Rice ....

2 medium pieces raw wakame

2 1/2 cups warm water

2 tablespoons chopped raw dulse

1/2 medium onion, minced

2 large garlic cloves, chopped

1 cup Germinated Brown Rice (page 131)

1 teaspoon unpasteurized raw barley miso

1 teaspoon raw sesame oil

Himalayan salt

Cayenne

Rinse the wakame, and soak it in the 2 1/2 cups warm water for 5 to 10 minutes. Squeeze out the water, and chop the wakame.

While the wakame is soaking, chop the dulse, onion, and garlic, and place in a large mixing bowl. Stir in the rice, miso, oil, and chopped wakame. Season with salt and cayenne to taste. Let stand for 35 to 45 minutes before serving to allow the flavors to blend.

Hearty Salad ....

This is makes a very high-nutrient dish when served with Germinated Brown Rice (page 131).

2 cups cherry tomatoes, cut in half

1 cup raw corn kernels

2 to 4 carrots, shredded

2 celery stalks, chopped

1 head broccoli, cut into bite-size pieces

1 bunch spinach leaves

1 red bell pepper, cut into julienne

1/2 jicama, shredded

1/2 purple onion, diced

1/2 cup green peas

2 tablespoons raw hemp oil

1 tablespoon Hunza black salt

1 tablespoon raw apple cider vinegar

1/2 teaspoon cayenne

Combine all the ingredients in a large salad bowl. Adjust the salt to taste.

High-Protein Wrap .... YIELD: 5 TO 6 SERVINGS

6 to 8 ripe avocados

3 to 4 cups finely chopped lettuce

3 to 4 cups finely chopped spinach

1 cup raw hempseeds

10 to 12 cherry tomatoes, chopped

3 to 4 green onions, sliced

¼ purple onion, finely chopped

7 to 10 pitted raw olives, chopped

3 cilantro sprigs, finely chopped

1 to 2 garlic cloves, finely chopped

1 to 2 fresh basil leaves, finely chopped

½ red jalapeño chile, seeded and finely chopped

¼ teaspoon ground cinnamon

¼ teaspoon Celtic sea salt

Dash of paprika

1 lemon

Collard leaves, lettuce leaves, or raw nori sheets

Set aside 4 of the avocados. Cut the remaining avocados into cubes, and place them in a large mixing bowl. Add the chopped lettuce, spinach, hempseeds, cherry tomatoes, green onions, onion, olives, cilantro, garlic, basil, chile, cinnamon, salt, and paprika. Mash the reserved avocados, and add them to the bowl. Squeeze the juice from the lemon directly into the bowl. Mix until everything is thoroughly combined. Wrap the mixture in collard leaves, lettuce leaves, or nori sheets, and serve.

NOTE: To heighten the heat and spicy taste, serve with Sambal Olek (page 154) on the side.

Holiday Vegetable Loaf ....

This loaf goes over very well at festive occasions and easily takes the place of animal-based dishes traditionally used for such events.

1½ cups Sunflower Pâté (page 165)

3 cups raw corn kernels

7 to 8 carrots, coarsely chopped

2 cups spinach

2 cups raw cashews

½ cup chopped onions

½ cup green onions

3 celery stalks, coarsely chopped

6 to 10 mushrooms

1 tablespoon chopped fresh sage

1 tablespoon minced fresh marjoram

1 tablespoon minced fresh rosemary

1 tablespoon minced fresh tarragon

1 to 2 garlic cloves, chopped

3 tablespoons Nama Shoyu

2 tablespoons freshly squeezed lemon juice

2 tablespoons raw olive oil (optional)

Combine the Sunflower Pâté, corn, carrots, spinach, cashews, onions, green onions, celery, mushrooms, sage, marjoram, rosemary, tarragon, and garlic in a large mixing bowl. Put the mixture through the hopper of a masticating or twin-gear juicer with the blank screen in place. (It might be necessary to repeat this process.) Transfer to a large bowl and add the Nama Shoyu, lemon juice, and optional olive oil to taste. Mix thoroughly using clean hands or gloves, if necessary. Form into a loaf. Serve as is, or drizzle with additional olive oil and dehydrate at 105 to 108 degrees F for 4 to 6 hours before serving.

NOTES: If desired, serve the fresh or dehydrated loaf with your favorite sauce from this book.

• If the loaf doesn't hold together well, you may wish to add some ground raw sunflower seeds or flaxseeds as a thickening agent.

Holiday Wild Rice ....

This makes for a very festive meal at holiday time.

1 cup wild rice, soaked until soft

2 cups shredded winter squash

4 green onions, sliced

2 shiitake mushrooms, chopped

1 tomato, diced (use only if in season)

½ cup chopped fresh cilantro

¼ cup sun-dried tomatoes, soaked

2 tablespoons Nama Shoyu

1 tablespoon freshly squeezed lemon juice

1½ teaspoons cumin seeds

1½ teaspoons chili powder

1 teaspoon turmeric

1 garlic clove

1 cup slivered raw almonds or walnuts

1 cup currants or mulberries

½ cup goji berries

¼ cup raw coconut oil

1 tablespoon raw walnut oil or pine nut oil

Cilantro sprigs, for garnish

Cranberries, for garnish

Soak the rice for about 4 days, changing the water twice daily, until it is soft and fluffy. Toss the drained rice with the squash, green onions, mushrooms, tomato, and cilantro in a large bowl.

Blend the sun-dried tomatoes, Nama Shoyu, lemon juice, cumin, chili powder, turmeric, and garlic in a high-powered blender to make a paste. Add this paste to the rice mixture, and mix well. Add the almonds, currants, goji berries, coconut oil, and walnut oil. Mix again. Garnish with cilantro sprigs and cranberries on the side of the serving dish.

Brown Rice Pilaf ....

PILAF

2 cups Germinated Brown Rice (below)

1 cup sweet cherry tomatoes, cut in half

3 red bell peppers, thinly sliced

1/3 cup chopped fresh Italian flat leaf parsley

SAUCE (makes about 1/2 cup)

1/3 cup raw olive oil

1/4 cup freshly squeezed lemon juice

1 tablespoon paprika

1 teaspoon sumac (see note)

1/2 garlic clove, crushed

Celtic sea salt, to taste

To make the pilaf, soak the germinated brown rice overnight. Rinse well. Place in a medium mixing bowl. Add the tomatoes, red bell peppers, and parsley, and set aside while you make the sauce.

For the sauce, combine all the ingredients in a high-powered blender, and process on low speed. Pour over the pilaf and toss. Refrigerate for a few hours before serving, tossing occasionally.

NOTE: Sumac is a Middle Eastern spice.

Germinated Brown Rice ....

This rice is delicious and feels very fortifying in the winter when mixed with Kimchee (page 69) or Sambal Olek (page 154). It also becomes a familiar dish reminiscent of cooked food when served with any of the bean and chili dishes found in this book.

2 cups germinated brown rice (see note)   1 1/4 to 1 1/2 cups water

Soak the rice in the water for 8 to 12 hours. Rinse well, drain, and serve.

NOTE: Germinated brown rice is packaged in Japan and sold through different distributors around the world. Please refer to the Resources section (pages 19–20) for suppliers in North America.

Israeli Eggplant .... Yield: 6 to 7 servings

1 to 2 eggplants

2 cups lightly salted water

1 cup chopped tomatoes

¼ teaspoon Celtic sea salt

½ cup diced onions

3 to 4 tablespoons freshly squeezed lemon juice

2 tablespoons raw tahini

4 garlic cloves, crushed

1 tablespoon raw olive oil

1 teaspoon chopped fresh mint

¼ teaspoon Celtic sea salt

Dash of cayenne

Curly parsley, for garnish

Use a toothpick, barbecue stick, or a fork to pierce holes along the entire length of the eggplant. Soak the eggplant in the salted water for 8 to 12 hours to remove the bitterness.

Put the eggplant in the sun or in a dehydrator for 4 to 5 hours. If the eggplant is still bitter, remove the skin. Squeeze the pulp to remove the bitter juices, and cut the eggplant into small pieces. Transfer to a food processor fitted with the S blade, and process into a purée. Add the tomatoes, onions, lemon juice, tahini, and garlic, and process until well combined.

Transfer to a serving bowl and add the olive oil, mint, salt, and cayenne. Mix thoroughly. Adjust the seasonings to taste. Let stand for 15 to 30 minutes before serving to allow the flavors to blend. Garnish with parsley.

Lentil Burgers .... YIELD: 5 OR 6 BURGERS

This burger is a favorite with men, especially when it is dehydrated.

3 cups lentils, sprouted

1 tablespoon raw pine nuts, soaked

1 tablespoon raw cashews, soaked

1 carrot, diced

1 tablespoon freshly squeezed lemon juice

1½ teaspoons Nama Shoyu

1½ teaspoons cayenne

1½ teaspoons curry powder

1 teaspoon chopped fresh sage (optional)

1 teaspoon Allspice (page 169)

Place the lentil sprouts in a medium mixing bowl. Grind the pine nuts and cashews in a mill, coffee grinder, or food processor fitted with the S blade, and add them to the sprouts. Add all the remaining ingredients. Mix and form into burgers. Serve at once or dehydrate at 105 to 108 degrees F for 4 hours. Turn over and dehydrate for another 4 hours. Serve straight from the dehydrator.

NOTES: These burgers are great served between two lettuce leaves.

• Enjoy these burgers with any of the condiments and sauces in this book. Also try them with Cheezy Tortilla Rolls (page 116).

Marinated Summer Squash with Watercress .... Yield: 4 to 5 servings

1 lemon

4 summer squashes (2 yellow, 2 green), finely sliced

4 tablespoons raw olive oil

1 tablespoon chopped chives

Celtic sea salt

Dash of ground nutmeg

Cayenne

2 large bunches watercress

2 tablespoons raw pine nuts

Finely grate the lemon peel and juice the lemon. Place in a bowl along with the squashes, olive oil, and chives. Season with salt, nutmeg, and cayenne to taste, and mix well. Marinate for 2 to 3 hours (at room temperature or in the refrigerator, depending on the climate).

Add the watercress and pine nuts, and mix well. Let rest for 15 to 20 minutes before serving.

Napa Spring Rolls .... Yield: 6 to 8 servings

Serve these spring rolls with Raw Mustard (page 160) on the side.

3 cups shredded napa cabbage

1/3 cup dry white wine (optional)

1 cup shredded carrots

1/2 cup chopped sweet onions

1/4 cup chopped fresh mint

12 to 16 shiitake mushrooms (2 for each roll), cut into thin strips

2 to 3 tablespoons Nama Shoyu

1 1/2 teaspoons raw black sesame seeds, soaked

1 teaspoon raw sesame oil

1/4 teaspoon paprika or chili powder

1 teaspoon crushed garlic

1 teaspoon crushed fresh ginger

6 to 8 raw rice paper sheets

Combine all the ingredients, except the rice paper, in a bowl. Marinate in the refrigerator for 8 to 12 hours. Roll the mixture in the rice paper.

Mock Chopped Liver ....

This is the raw vegan version of chopped liver traditionally served at Passover or Rosh Hashanah. It will surprise and delight your family and friends.

6 ounces fresh mushrooms, wiped clean and thinly sliced

1 large, sweet onion, diced

1 cup raw walnuts

½ cup raw almonds

1 large garlic clove, minced

½ cup raw hemp oil or olive oil

Dash of raw apple cider vinegar

2 tablespoons Nama Shoyu

¼ teaspoon chili powder

Dash of cayenne

Dash of Hunza black salt

7 to 8 cherry tomatoes

2 to 3 watercress sprigs

1 parsley sprig

Place the mushrooms, onion, walnuts, almonds, and garlic in a food processor fitted with the S blade, and pulse until chopped. Add the oil and vinegar to taste, and pulse until thoroughly combined. Add the Nama Shoyu, chili powder, cayenne, and salt, and pulse again until evenly mixed.

Transfer to a large serving bowl and cover tightly. Refrigerate for 2 to 3 hours or longer. Remove from the refrigerator and allow to rest at room temperature for about 30 minutes before serving. Garnish with the cherry tomatoes, watercress, and parsley.

NOTE: This recipe may be made a day in advance. Garnish just before serving.

Mushroom Burgers .... YIELD: 1 TO 2 SERVINGS

This recipe is a favorite with children and is very easy to make.

2 portobello mushrooms

2 tablespoons raw apple cider vinegar or umeboshi vinegar

1 tablespoon raw olive oil

1 tablespoon Nama Shoyu

1 garlic clove

1 very ripe tomato, sliced

½ cucumber, thinly sliced

¼ cup pitted raw olives, finely chopped

1 yellow bell pepper, finely chopped

1 red bell pepper, finely chopped

1 handful sprouts

½ red onion, thinly sliced

1 tablespoon raw sea vegetable flakes (optional)

1 tablespoon raw capers

Clean the mushrooms and cut off the stems. Put the whole mushrooms in a dish. Combine the vinegar, oil, Nama Shoyu, and garlic in a high-powered blender, and process until well blended. Pour over the mushrooms. Place in a dehydrator at 105 degrees F for 1 to 2 hours. On the inside of 1 mushroom, build a tower of the tomato, cucumber, olives, bell peppers, sprouts, onions, sea vegetable flakes, and capers. Serve as is, or cover with the other mushroom., press down, and serve with a drizzle of juice from the tomatoes on the side.

NOTES: Use a mandoline to slice the cucumbers into very thin strips.

• The addition of the sea vegetable flakes gives this recipe a great nutritional boost and is a creative way of adding sea vegetables to children's diets. To make your own flakes, simply tear raw nori sheets into tiny strips (children love doing this) and add kelp granules or dulse.

Peppery Hempfredo Touch Al Dente

YIELD: ABOUT 4 SERVINGS

2 medium zucchinis

2 cups raw hempseeds (hulled)

2 lemons, juiced

3 teaspoons unpasteurized raw miso
  or Nama Shoyu

1 teaspoon raw hemp oil or olive oil

3 fresh sage leaves

½ teaspoon peppercorns (optional)

1 garlic clove

1 rosemary sprig

Finely shred the zucchinis into "noodles" with a spiral slicer (page 18). To make a sauce, combine the remaining ingredients in a high-powered blender, and process until creamy. Alternatively, process the ingredients through the hopper of a twin gear juicer, and then blend them into a creamy paste with a spoon. Pour over the zucchini noodles and serve.

Quinoa Delight ....

YIELD: 2 TO 4 SERVINGS

2 cups quinoa, sprouted

1 medium red or orange pepper,
  minced

1 cup thinly sliced arugula

1 cup thinly sliced bok choy

½ cup raw dulse pieces

¼ cup finely chopped fresh basil

1 teaspoon Nama Shoyu

Combine all the ingredients and mix well. Let stand for about 1 hour (at room temperature or in the refrigerator, depending on the climate) before serving.

Raw Spaghetti .... YIELD: 4 TO 6 SERVINGS

You'll have the most success with this recipe if you use a spiral slicer (see page 18).

2 to 3 zucchinis, made into "noodles" with a spiral slicer or very thinly sliced

1 cup Alfredo Pasta Sauce (page 150)

2 red bell peppers, finely chopped

3 to 4 green onions, finely chopped

Put the zucchini in a bowl and pour the sauce over it. Garnish with the bell peppers and green onions before serving.

NOTES: This recipe also works well with Herbed "Ricotta Cheese" (page 155) or any of the other sauces in this book.

• If zucchinis are not available, use any other squash you prefer.

Raw Burrito .... YIELD: 2 TO 3 SERVINGS

This rich and filling dish takes some advance preparation, so be sure to allow plenty of time. It is well worth the effort and is extremely popular with those who are new to raw vegan cuisine.

1 recipe High-Protein Wrap, using 2 or 3 collard leaves (page 128)

Marinade of your choice

1/4 cup "Cheese" Sauce (page 150)

1 to 2 cups Marinara Sauce (page 157)

Trim and discard the bottom stems of the collard leaves, and soak the leaves in your favorite marinade until softened. Drain the leaves, and wrap the filling in them. Pour the "Cheese" Sauce over the wraps, then pour the Marinara Sauce on top. Serve immediately.

VARIATION: If you prefer, Cheezy Tortilla Rolls (page 116) may be used as wrappers in place of the collard greens.

Raw Vegan Sushi .... YIELD: 3 TO 4 SERVINGS

This is very popular at parties.

2 to 3 ripe avocados, thinly sliced

1 to 2 tablespoons freshly squeezed lemon juice, plus additional as needed

1 to 2 bunches spinach leaves

7 to 10 raw nori sheets

2 cucumbers, seeds removed, sliced into matchsticks

1 red bell pepper, sliced into matchsticks

1 cup bean sprouts

Nama Shoyu

Put the avocado slices in a small bowl and sprinkle with the lemon juice. Place 2 or 3 spinach leaves on each nori sheet. Layer on a small amount of the cucumbers, followed by a layer of red bell pepper, and a layer of bean sprouts. Place 2 or 3 avocado slices on top, and roll up the nori sheet tightly using a bamboo mat, if available.

Seal the edge of the rolls with lemon juice. Just prior to serving, cut the rolls in half and arrange them on a platter. Serve with Nama Shoyu in small saucers as a dipping sauce.

VARIATION: Instead of Nama Shoyu, use any of the sauces in this book as a dipping sauce.

Spicy Seaweed Roll .... YIELD: ABOUT 6 SERVINGS

This dish is wildly popular with those who love hot and spicy Thai and Indonesian cuisine.

8 to 12 raw nori sheets

1 cup grated parsnips

1 cup grated carrots

1 white onion, diced

4 to 5 tablespoons raw coconut milk

1 stalk lemongrass, finely chopped

1 red chile, seeded and diced

1 tablespoon Nama Shoyu

1 slice fresh ginger

Dash of Celtic sea salt

1 cup bean sprouts

4 cucumbers, seeded and cut into julienne

5 to 7 mint sprigs

Raw sesame oil

1½ cups Sambal Olek (page 154)

Put a nori sheet on a bamboo sushi mat and set aside. Place the parsnips and carrots in a bowl and toss them together. Place the onion, coconut milk, lemongrass, chile, Nama Shoyu, ginger, and salt in a high-powered blender, and process until well combined. Pour over the parsnips and carrots, and let marinate for about 30 minutes.

Drain the carrots and parsnips, but reserve the liquid. Be sure to squeeze out all the moisture. Transfer the parsnips and carrots to a dry bowl. Put the marinade liquid in tiny individual saucers, and put one drop of sesame oil in each one.

Take a small amount of the parsnips and carrots and some of the bean sprouts, cucumbers, and mint, and place on a nori sheet. Roll into tubes and cut in half. Arrange the rolls on a platter. Put a drop or two of the Sambal Olek on top of each roll and serve the remainder along with the marinade liquid as a dipping sauce.

Stir-Frei (Be Free!) Pad Thai

4 zucchinis

2 cucumbers

⅓ cup raw hemp oil

1 lemon, juiced

1 tablespoons chopped fresh ginger

3 pitted raw black olives

1½ teaspoons tamarind

1 teaspoon coriander seeds

1 garlic clove

1 tablespoon Nama Shoyu

1 medium tomato, sliced

1 handful cremini mushrooms, quartered

1 parsley sprig

1 red bell pepper, sliced into rings

Finely shred the zucchinis and cucumbers into "noodles" with a spiral slicer (page 18). Combine the oil, lemon juice, ginger, olives, tamarind, coriander seeds, and garlic in a high-powered blender, and process until smooth. Pour over the shredded vegetables and toss gently. Add Nama Shoyu to taste, and toss gain. Garnish with the tomato and mushrooms. Place the parsley sprig and red bell pepper rings on the side.

Stuffed Tomatoes .... YIELD: 4 SERVINGS

4 large tomatoes

½ cup chopped fresh basil

1 tablespoon chopped fresh oregano

1 tablespoon minced fresh tarragon

1 teaspoon Celtic sea salt

½ teaspoon chopped fresh thyme

½ teaspoon cayenne

3 cups raw sunflower seeds

1 cup raw pumpkin seeds

1 cup sun-dried tomatoes, soaked

6 to 8 pitted raw olives, minced

1 garlic clove

1 teaspoon freshly squeezed lemon juice

1 bunch sunflower or green pea sprouts

1 tablespoon raw olive oil

Slice the top off the tomatoes making very smooth slices, and set aside. Scoop out the seeds and most of the flesh of the tomatoes, and place in a bowl. Add the basil, oregano, tarragon, salt, thyme, and cayenne to the tomato pulp, and set aside.

Place the sunflower seeds and pumpkin seeds in a high-powered blender or food processor fitted with the S blade, and grind until powdery. Add the sun-dried tomatoes along with some of the soak water, olives, garlic and lemon juice, and process well. Put into the bowl with the tomato pulp and mix thoroughly. Use this mixture to stuff the tomatoes until they are completely full, and cover with the reserved tomato tops.

Arrange the sprouts on a platter, and place the stuffed tomatoes on top. Drizzle with the olive oil and serve.

Thai Coconut Curry .... YIELD: 2 TO 4 SERVINGS

SALAD

2 medium celery stalks, thinly sliced

1 medium zucchini, shredded

1 medium carrot, shredded

1 medium bok choy, thinly sliced

1 medium red bell pepper, thinly sliced

½ cup sliced mushrooms

1 to 2 medium green onions, thinly sliced

SAUCE

1 medium, young Thai coconut, water and flesh

½ to ⅓ cup raw pine nuts

1 tablespoon curry powder

1 tablespoon chopped fresh ginger

1 tablespoon thinly sliced lemongrass

2 to 3 teaspoons Thai chili paste (optional)

2 medium garlic cloves (optional)

¼ to ½ teaspoon dry mustard

Combine the salad ingredients in a bowl. Combine the sauce ingredients in a high-powered blender, and process until smooth and creamy. Pour three-quarters of the sauce over the salad, and toss well. Reserve the remaining sauce to serve as a condiment on the side.

Veggie Balls ....

These tasty balls make a great meal for entertaining meat eaters and anyone who is skeptical of a raw vegan diet.

2 cups raw sunflower seeds, ground

2 cups carrots, shredded

1 cup chopped zucchini

½ cup finely chopped onions

3 bunches green onions, chopped

2 tablespoons nutritional yeast (optional)

2 tablespoons Nama Shoyu

1 teaspoon curry powder

½ cup celery juice

Rich Curry Sauce (page 164) or Alfredo Pasta Sauce (page 150)

Combine the sunflower seeds, carrots, zucchini, onions, green onions, optional nutritional yeast, Nama Shoyu, and curry powder in a food processor fitted with the S blade. Gradually add the celery juice, and process into a moist dough. Roll into 1-inch balls using moistened hands (or coat your hands with raw olive oil). Place on a dehydrator tray (without a Teflex sheet) and dehydrate at 110 to 115 degrees F for 12 to 24 hours, turning the balls over at least once midway in the cycle. Serve with the sauce of your choice.

Zucchi-Ghetti with Marinara Sauce

YIELD: ABOUT 4 SERVINGS

ZUCCI-GHETTI

2 medium zucchinis

SAUCE

2 cups chopped tomatoes

¾ cup raw hemp oil

½ cup sun-dried tomatoes, soaked

¼ cup Nama Shoyu

¼ cup chopped fresh basil

¼ cup chopped fresh oregano

5 pitted sun-dried raw olives

2 tablespoons raw hempseeds

½ lemon, juiced

1 tablespoon minced garlic

1 hot chile

1 teaspoon peeled and chopped fresh ginger

GARNISH

Spearmint leaves

Diced red bell peppers

Diced tomatoes

Watercress leaves

Finely shred the zucchini into "noodles" using a spiral slicer (page 18). Combine all the sauce ingredients in a high-powdered blender, and process until smooth. Pour over the zucchini and toss well. Garnish with spearmint leaves, red bell peppers, and tomatoes on top. Place watercress leaves on the side.

Spiced Pears and Red Cabbage

This is a simple, warming dish that most children can make in the winter months with a little assistance from you.

4 cups finely sliced red cabbage (about 1 medium head)

2 winter pears, peeled, cored, and chopped

¼ cup raw apple cider vinegar

¼ cup agave nectar

1 teaspoon Ground Lemon Peel (page 169)

½ teaspoon caraway seeds

½ teaspoon Celtic sea salt

¼ teaspoon cayenne

¼ teaspoon Allspice (page 169)

¼ teaspoon ground cinnamon

Place the cabbage and pears in a medium mixing bowl. Add the remaining ingredients, and mix well. Let stand for about 1 hour to allow the flavors to blend. Mix again before serving.

Avocado Sandwich .... YIELD: 3 TO 4 SERVINGS

For a very simple and quick meal, make enough salsa beforehand so you will have it ready.

2 tablespoon Salsa (page 161)

1 ripe avocado

4 to 5 leaves romaine lettuce

Pour the salsa into a bowl. Finely chop the avocado, add it to the salsa, and mix thoroughly. Spread on the lettuce leaves and serve.

Avocado Spread Sandwich .... YIELD: 4 TO 5 SERVINGS

This is a very easy way to incorporate the health-giving properties of pumpkin seeds into your diet. This recipe is high in nutrients and simple to prepare.

1 large, very ripe avocado, cut into chunks

½ cup raw pumpkin seeds

¼ cup water

2 tablespoons freshly squeezed lemon juice

1 teaspoon Nama Shoyu or Celtic sea salt

1 tablespoon caraway seeds

Dash of cayenne

Lettuce leaves

Place the avocado in a high-powered blender. Add the pumpkins seeds, 2 tablespoons of the water, and all the lemon juice, and process on medium speed. Add more water only if needed to facilitate blending and achieve the desired consistency. Add the caraway seeds, Nama Shoyu, and cayenne to taste, and pulse until blended. Spread on the lettuce leaves and serve.

Spicy Nut Sandwich .... YIELD: 2 SERVINGS

This meal is packed with nutrients.

2 collard leaves

6 tablespoons Sunflower Pâté (page 165)

6 to 8 tablespoons Salsa (page 161)

Cut the stem off the end of the collard leaves. Spread a generous portion of the pâté on each leaf. Top with the salsa. Wrap and serve.

Savory Pie Crust ....

Stuff this crust with any of the savory spreads in this book.

1¼ cups raw almonds

1 cup chopped dates

1 tablespoon finely chopped fresh basil

½ teaspoon Celtic sea salt

½ teaspoon Italian seasoning mix

1 tablespoon celery juice

2 teaspoons psyllium husk powder

Chop the almonds in a food processor fitted with the S blade until they are coarsely ground. Add the dates, and process until the almonds are finely ground. Add the basil, salt, and seasoning mix. Gradually add the celery juice. The crust must be slightly damp and holding together before the psyllium is added. Gradually add the psyllium. Press the mixture into an 8- or 9-inch pie plate, and either place it in the sun for 1 to 2 hours or in a dehydrator at 103 to 105 degrees F for about 1 hour. Use immediately.

NOTE: For longer storage, this crust may be frozen.

Sauces, Spreads, Dips, and Condiments

In this chapter you'll find many recipes that will enhance your favorite raw foods and will help you make delicious, attractive, enticing meals. Sauces are especially wonderful on raw "noodles" or any raw vegetables. Spreads can be used for quick sandwiches when layered between lettuce or dark leafy greens. You can even make canapés using the spreads on raw crackers. Dips are always great for crudités, of course, or with raw vegan crackers or chips. The condiments are tasty additions to many of the recipes in this book, so prepare them in advance and keep them handy.

Alfredo Pasta Sauce .... YIELD: 1 CUP

Serve with Raw Spaghetti (page 138) or your favorite raw "noodles."

1 cup raw cashews

1 handful fresh oregano, minced

1 small onion, minced

¼ cup celery juice

1 tablespoon raw pine nuts

1 to 2 garlic cloves, minced

Dash of Celtic sea salt

Combine all the ingredients in a high-powered blender, and process until smooth.

"Cheese" Sauce .... YIELD: 2 TO 3 CUPS

A favorite with children, this recipe may be used as a sauce or spread.

2 cups raw cashews

2 cups water

2 cups chopped tomatoes

1 cup chopped red bell peppers

½ cup nutritional yeast

½ cup freshly squeezed lemon juice

¼ cup minced purple onions

¼ cup germinated raw sesame seeds

4 teaspoons paprika

1 teaspoon Celtic sea salt

2 garlic cloves

½ cup raw olive oil

Combine the cashews, water, tomatoes, bell peppers, nutritional yeast, lemon juice, onions, sesame seeds, paprika, salt, and garlic in a high-powered blender, gradually going from low to high speed until the mixture has a cheeselike texture. Drizzle in the olive oil on low speed (through the cap opening in the lid) until well combined.

NOTE: This recipe may be made two days in advance and stored in the refrigerator.

Hemp Pesto ....

Enjoy this pesto tossed with Raw Spaghetti (page 138).

2 cups raw hempseeds

2 cups fresh basil

⅓ cup unpasteurized raw miso or
    Nama Shoyu

2 tablespoons raw hemp oil

2 teaspoons raw tahini

3 pitted sun-dried raw olives

2 garlic cloves

Process all the ingredients in a twin-gear juicer or high-powered blender, or grind them in a mortar with a pestle.

NOTE: If desired, garnish with a basil crown and chive flowers.

Pesto ....

This sauce can be added to soups or mixed with Raw Spaghetti (page 138). Serve it at parties as a dip. It is especially appealing to preteens and teenagers.

5 large garlic cloves

Dash of coarse Celtic sea salt

2 cups packed fresh basil, washed well
    and spun dry

½ cup Herbed "Ricotta Cheese" (page
    155; optional)

⅓ cup raw olive oil

Place the garlic and salt in a large mortar, and pound it vigorously into a paste using a pestle. Add the basil gradually, and grind it into a dark paste. Add the optional Herbed "Ricotta Cheese" in 4 batches, and pound it until the mixture is the consistency of soft butter. Gradually beat in the oil until the sauce has the consistency of coarse mayonnaise.

Date Butter .... YIELD: 3 CUPS

2 to 3 cups pitted dates
½ cup water, as needed

Place the dates in a high-powered blender, using just enough water to moisten the dates and make a thick, spreadable paste. Mix well, pulsing at intervals and using a spatula to scrape down the sides of the blender jar. Use a plunger to keep the mixture moving. Be very patient with this procedure. Add more water as necessary until the desired consistency is achieved.

Pear Honey Butter .... YIELD: 2 TO 3 CUPS

This sweet, creamy butter is terrific spread on celery sticks or lettuce leaves. The addition of camu camu powder gives it a vitamin C boost. Serve this if your child has the flu. It is also great to give children and their friends when they have a pajama party or are visiting after school.

4½ pounds ripe Bartlett pears

3 cups pitted dates

2 cups raw honey

2 tablespoons freshly squeezed lemon juice

½ teaspoon grated lemon peel

½ teaspoon ground ginger

½ teaspoon ground cinnamon

¼ teaspoon ground nutmeg

1 tablespoon camu camu powder (optional)

Peel, core, and chop the pears. Place them in a high-powered blender or a food processor fitted with the S blade. Add the dates, honey, lemon juice, lemon peel, ginger, cinnamon, and nutmeg, and process into a smooth purée. Add the camu camu powder and mix again. Ladle into clean jars, seal, and store in the refrigerator.

Fermented Pickles ....

4 to 8 tablespoons dill seeds

8 bay leaves

2 tablespoons mustard seeds

2 tablespoons peppercorns

2 tablespoons whole allspice

10 garlic cloves

4 to 8 dried red chiles

1 tablespoon turmeric

2 bunches fresh dill

20 to 24 pickling cucumbers (3 to 3½ pounds)

2 quarts water

¼ cup coarse Celtic sea salt or Himalayan salt

¼ cup raw apple cider vinegar or umeboshi vinegar

Place half of the spices and half of the dill on the bottom of a large Mason jar, glass jar, stone crock, or stainless steel container. Add half of the cucumbers. Top with the remaining spices, dill, and cucumbers. Combine the water, salt, and vinegar. Mix well and cover the cucumbers with this brine. Make sure the cucumbers are fully covered and remain under the brine. Store the container in a cool place (70 to 80 degrees F).

Check the container often, and promptly removing any scum or mold that might be forming on top. When the pickles are fully fermented, store them in the refrigerator, making sure that they are always covered with the brine.

NOTES: The pickles may be kept at lower temperatures, but they will take longer to fully ferment. Temperatures above 80 degrees F may cause spoilage, so check them every day.

• If the cucumbers become soft and slimy or give off a foul odor, discard them and start again from scratch.

Sambal Olek #1 ....

This Indonesian-inspired chili paste is a great way to store excess chiles that you may have harvested. It is ready to use whenever chiles are needed for a recipe.

25 chiles

1 tablespoon raw apple cider vinegar

2 teaspoons grey sea salt

Wash the chiles. Remove the stems but not the seeds. Place the whole chiles in a high-powered blender. Add about $1\frac{1}{2}$ teaspoons of the vinegar, and process into a paste.

If the paste is too thick and chunky, add a little more vinegar, then process again until smooth. Add the salt and process again. Store the chili paste in a sterilized airtight jar in the refrigerator.

NOTE: Do not lift the lid straight off the blender jar to look inside, as you might get a huge, unpleasant whiff of chile fumes. Let the paste settle before carefully opening the lid.

Sambal Olek #2 .... YIELD: 1 CUP

½ cup finely chopped hot chiles

2 tablespoons freshly squeezed lime juice

2 tablespoons raw sesame oil

½ teaspoon Himalayan salt

Combine all the ingredients in a high-powered blender, and process into a smooth paste. Store in a sterilized airtight jar in the refrigerator.

Herbed "Ricotta Cheese" .... YIELD: ABOUT 2 CUPS

1 cup raw cashews

1 cup water, more or less as needed

½ cup raw macadamia nuts

2 tablespoons raw pine nuts

2 teaspoons freshly squeezed lemon juice

1 teaspoon chopped fresh basil

1 teaspoon chopped fresh dill

1 teaspoon chopped fresh oregano

1 teaspoon palm nectar (optional, but highly recommended)

½ teaspoon Celtic sea salt

Combine all the ingredients in a high-powered blender or food processor fitted with the S blade, and process until smooth. Add more water as needed to achieve the desired consistency. Transfer to a glass bowl, cover with a moist terry cloth or towel, and let stand at room temperature for about 6 hours. Refrigerate before serving.

Herb Butter .... YIELD: ABOUT 2 CUPS

Use this as a spread in place of butter, or as a stuffing (see Herbed Mushrooms, page 107). This recipe is a great way to keep an overabundance of herbs from spoiling, and is very convenient to have on hand for flavoring various recipes.

1 bunch fresh cilantro, minced

1 bunch fresh marjoram, minced

1 bunch fresh dill, minced

1 bunch fresh tarragon, minced

1 bunch fresh parsley, minced

1 bunch fresh sorrel, minced

Put the minced herbs in a mixing bowl, or use a mortar and pestle, and add just enough water to make a paste. Mix well. Freeze in plastic ice cube trays. As soon as the cubes are frozen, transfer them to a freezer-safe storage container. Stored in the freezer, Herb Butter will keep for several months.

NOTE: When you need to make an herb spread or butter, defrost the number of cubes needed and add raw olive oil and Celtic sea salt or Nama Shoyu according to your desired taste.

Looks-Like-Dairy Dip .... YIELD: 1 CUP

This dip is great to take to parties with a tray of crudités surrounding it.

1 cup raw cashews

2 tablespoons minced fresh dill

2 tablespoons celery juice

1½ to 2 teaspoons nutritional yeast

1½ teaspoons freshly squeezed lemon
    juice

½ teaspoon ground ginger

½ garlic clove (optional)

Celtic sea salt

Dash of paprika

Combine the cashews, dill, celery juice, nutritional yeast, lemon juice, ginger, optional garlic, and salt to taste in a high-powered blender or food processor fitted with the S blade. Process until smooth, adding a very small amount of water or additional celery juice if necessary. Transfer to a serving bowl. Garnish with the paprika. Serve with raw vegetables or crackers.

NOTE: This dip becomes thicker when refrigerated. Keeping it chilled will help it stay fresher longer for parties.

Creamy Avocado Dip .... YIELD: 4 TO 5 SERVINGS

This recipe is very handy for entertaining. Place it in a serving bowl surrounded with crudités

1 large ripe avocado, cut into chunks

1 tablespoon Vegan Herb Mayonnaise
    (page 167)

1 tablespoon freshly squeezed lemon
    juice

½ teaspoon Celtic sea salt

1 garlic clove, minced

¼ teaspoon cayenne

Combine all the ingredients in a high-powered blender or food processor fitted with the S blade, and process into a smooth purée.

Marinade Sauce ....

This is the perfect solution for softening tough cruciferous vegetables.

½ to ¾ cup Nama Shoyu

2 to 3 lemons, juiced

½ cup raw olive oil

¼ cup raw apple cider vinegar

½ teaspoon cayenne (optional)

Combine all the ingredients in a bottle. Seal tightly, and shake until well blended.

Marinara Sauce .... YIELD: ABOUT 2 CUPS

This is an extremely popular sauce and always surprises those who are new to raw cuisine. Serve it over Raw Spaghetti (page 138) or your favorite raw vegetable "noodles."

1 to 2 cups very ripe tomatoes

½ cup sun-dried tomatoes, ground

½ cup celery juice

1 handful fresh oregano, minced

1 handful fresh thyme, minced

2 to 3 tablespoons freshly squeezed lemon juice

2 to 3 garlic cloves, crushed

Dash of Celtic sea salt

Dash of cayenne

Combine all the ingredients in a high-powered blender, and process until the desired consistency is achieved.

Coconut Kefir ....

3 to 4 young Thai coconuts

Open each husked coconut by holding it with the eyes facing down in your hand. Hit it with the back of a heavy knife in a circular manner until a round "lid" pops open. Pour out the coconut water. (Drink the coconut water immediately, or keep it refrigerated until you are ready to use it in another recipe.) Keep intact the coconut with the lid that is the cleanest and easiest to work with. If they all came out great, keep intact the one with the thinnest flesh.

Spoon out the flesh of the other coconuts. If the openings are not big enough for you to use a spoon, break them open all the way. To do this, hit the coconuts lengthwise with the back of your knife, or put them in a plastic bag and hit them on the ground. Fill the intact coconut with the flesh of the broken ones. Place the lid back on the coconut and wrap it with cellophane to keep it entirely airtight.

Let the coconut rest at room temperature for 1 to 3 days to allow the flesh to naturally ferment. (The number of days needed will depend on the ambient temperature; in warmer climates the fermentation will be faster.) Check the stage of fermentation daily. When the coconut kefir smells appetizing, it is ready to eat. If you cannot eat it immediately, store it for a day or two in the refrigerator.

NOTE: Only untreated coconuts will naturally ferment.

Mustard Seed Cream Sauce .... YIELD: 1 CUP

Use this as a dipping sauce or salad dressing.

½ cup vegetable broth or diluted, freshly made vegetable juice
½ cup raw cashews
1 teaspoon mustard seeds
1 teaspoon Dijon mustard
Dash of Celtic sea salt

Combine all the ingredients in a high-powered blender, and process until smooth and creamy. Pour into a glass jar, and cover until ready to use.

Olive Dip and Spread .... YIELD: 1 CUP

This spread is a favorite at parties with a tray of crudités surrounding it.

1 ripe avocado
1 tomato
6 to 8 pitted raw olives
1 garlic clove

Combine the avocado, tomato, and olives in a high-powered blender, and process until smooth and creamy. Gradually add the garlic to taste.

Raw Almond Butter ....

Use this spread for snacks and recipes that call for almond butter or any kind of nut or sweet butter.

1 cup raw almonds, soaked for 8 to 12 hours

¼ cup raw grapeseed oil, flaxseed oil, or almond oil

½ teaspoon agave nectar

½ teaspoon ground cinnamon

¼ teaspoon Celtic sea salt

Dash of almond extract

⅓ cup water (optional)

Rinse the almonds thoroughly, and drain well. Process them into a paste in a grinder, high-powered blender, or masticating juicer.

Combine the oil, agave nectar, cinnamon, salt, and almond extract in a bowl. Transfer to a high powered blender along with the almond paste, and process thoroughly, turning off the blender occasionally to scrape down the sides of the blender jar. You may need to add small amounts of water from time to time, or use a plunger to keep the mixture moving. Store in the refrigerator, and use as soon as possible.

Raw Mustard ....

1 cup raw apple cider vinegar

1 onion, chopped

3 to 5 tablespoons mustard seeds

1 to 3 tablespoons raw mustard oil

1 garlic clove, crushed

Dash of Celtic sea salt or Himalayan salt

Combine all the ingredients in a high-powered blender until the desired consistency is achieved. Turn off the blender occasionally to scrape down the sides of the blender jar, and use a plunger to keep the mixture moving. Adjust the ingredients according to your taste. Store in an airtight bottle in the refrigerator.

Salsa .... YIELD: 5 TO 6 SERVINGS

This recipe is great to make in advance to use with other recipes.

3 very ripe tomatoes

¼ onion, diced

2 tablespoons minced fresh cilantro

6 pitted raw olives, minced

3 to 4 fresh basil leaves, finely chopped

1 tablespoon freshly squeezed lemon juice

1 tablespoon chopped fresh mint

1 ripe jalapeño chile, or 1 teaspoon cayenne

¼ teaspoon Celtic sea salt

Combine all the ingredients in a medium bowl and toss. Let marinate for 1 to 2 hours (at room temperature or in the refrigerator, depending on the climate) before serving.

NOTE: If your budget is very tight, you can make a nutritious and delicious sandwich by wrapping a few spoonfuls of Salsa in a lettuce leaf.

Spicy Salsa .... YIELD: 4 TO 6 SERVINGS

1 large tomato, diced

1 medium red bell pepper, very finely diced

¼ cup minced red onions

2 tablespoons freshly squeezed lime juice

1 tablespoon raw olive oil

2 to 4 raw olives, chopped

2 teaspoons ground cumin

1 garlic clove, minced

1 teaspoon Mexican seasoning

1 teaspoon red jalapeño chile, seeded and minced

Dash of Celtic sea salt

2 tablespoons minced fresh cilantro

Combine the tomato, red bell pepper, onions, lime juice, oil, olives, cumin, garlic, Mexican seasoning, and chile in a bowl or jar, and mix well. Add salt to taste. Refrigerate for 1 to 2 hours. Add the cilantro just before serving.

Teenager's Party Salsa .... Yield: 5 to 6 servings

This is great for parties along with Ground Avocado (page 106). You can serve them together on celery sticks or wrapped in lettuce leaves.

5 serrano chiles

1 large garlic clove

3 large or 5 small, ripe tomatoes, chopped

1 teaspoon Celtic sea salt

¼ white onion, chopped

1 teaspoon Celtic sea salt

2 cilantro stems, chopped

Place the chiles and garlic in a mortar and use a pestle to grind them into small pieces. Add the tomatoes and grind them into a paste. Add the onion, salt, and cilantro, and mix well. Serve at room temperature or thoroughly chilled.

NOTE: The chile seeds are not hot; however, the veins are. If you prefer a mild salsa, remove the veins.

Cocomango Chutney .... Yield: 2 servings

1 young Thai coconut

1 lime, juiced

1 ripe mango, chopped

Scoop out the flesh from the coconut, and cut it into small chunks. Place it in a small mixing bowl, add the lime juice, and let marinate for 4 to 6 hours. Add the mango with just enough liquid (from both the coconut and the mango) to mash with a fork. Alternatively, pulse the mixture in a food processor fitted with the S blade or in a high-powered blender.

NOTE: If fresh mango is not available, soak ½ cup dried mangoes for 2 to 3 hours, and use in place of the fresh mango along with some of the soaking water. You will need to use a high-powered blender or food processor fitted with the S blade, and pulse the mixture to obtain the proper texture.

Pear Macadamia Nut Chutney

Instead of using a food processor to make this chutney, it might be fun to try a mortar and pestle.

3 tablespoons chopped onions

1 teaspoon minced fresh ginger

1 teaspoon minced garlic

1 teaspoon Ground Lemon Peel (page 169)

2 cups chopped pears

½ cup agave nectar

½ cup raw apple cider vinegar

½ cup chopped raw macadamia nuts

Combine the onions, ginger, garlic, and Ground Lemon Peel in a food processor fitted with the S blade, and process until ground and well blended. Alternatively, grind them with a mortar and pestle. Combine the pears, agave nectar, and apple cider vinegar in a large mixing bowl, and stir well until the pear is evenly coated. Add the onion mixture and stir until thick. Add the macadamia nuts, and mix until they are well distributed. Chill thoroughly before serving.

NOTE: Chutney is a very common condiment used throughout India and most of Asia. It is similar to the salsas eaten in Central and South America and the relishes served in Europe and North America. It can enhance a bland dish and is a very easy way to add extra nutrients to a meal. Although this recipe calls for a mortar and pestle as an alternative to a food processor, a suribachi can be used as well. A suribachi is the Japanese version of the mortar and pestle. It consists of an earthenware bowl that is glazed on the outside. The inside of the bowl is ridged to facilitate grinding. It is used with a wooden pestle called surikogi.

Rich Curry Sauce .... YIELD: 3 CUPS

1 cup raw cashews

¾ cup chopped fresh cilantro

½ cup chopped onions

3 tablespoons raw mustard oil (optional)

1 tablespoon Sambal Olek (page 154; optional)

2 garlic cloves

2 slices fresh ginger

1 teaspoon curry powder

1 teaspoon ground cumin

½ teaspoon turmeric

Dash of ground cinnamon

1 cup celery juice

Combine the cashews, cilantro, onions, optional mustard oil, optional Sambal Olek, garlic, ginger, curry powder, cumin, turmeric, and cinnamon in a high-powered blender. Add a portion of the celery juice, and begin processing. Gradually add more celery juice, as needed, until the desired consistency is achieved. Store in an airtight jar in the refrigerator.

Super Sprout Spread .... YIELD: 3 TO 4 CUPS

2 cups raw sunflower seeds, sprouted

1 cup green pea sprouts

1 bunch parsley, finely chopped

1 bunch fresh basil, finely chopped

1 small red or orange bell pepper, chopped

1½ medium lemons, juiced (rind optional)

1 tablespoon ground cumin

1 medium garlic clove

Dash of cayenne

Combine all the ingredients in a food processor fitted with the S blade, and process until evenly combined and the desired texture is achieved.

Sunflower Spread ....

This is a very hearty meal that is great for people on a budget. Wrap the spread in collard greens or lettuce leaves for a highly nutritious meal.

3 cups raw sunflower seeds, sprouted

¼ cup Nama Shoyu

2 to 3 garlic cloves, chopped

Dash of cayenne

1 cup freshly squeezed lemon juice

Combine the sprouts, Nama Shoyu, garlic, and cayenne in a food processor fitted with the S blade. Add the lemon juice gradually, according to your taste, and process until smooth. Stored in an airtight container in the refrigerator, Sunflower Spread will keep for up to 2 weeks.

NOTE: For a smoother spread, grind the sunflower seeds instead of sprouting them. Transfer to a food processor fitted with the S blade, add the other ingredients gradually.

Sunflower Pâté .... YIELD: 2 TO 3 CUPS

Use this pâté for Seaweed Chips (page 173).

1½ cups raw sunflower seeds, soaked

½ cup chopped onions

1 lemon, juiced

3 to 4 tablespoons Nama Shoyu

2 to 3 tablespoons peeled and
    chopped fresh ginger

2 to 3 garlic cloves

1 teaspoon cayenne

1 teaspoon curry powder

1 tablespoon raw olive oil

Combine the sunflower seeds, onions, lemon juice, Nama Shoyu, ginger, garlic, cayenne, and curry powder in a food processor fitted with the S blade or a high-powered blender, and process until very smooth. Add a small amount of water, only if necessary, to facilitate blending and achieve the desired consistency. Add the olive oil and mix thoroughly.

Sweet-and-Spicy Marinade .... YIELD: 2 CUPS

This recipe can be used as a dipping sauce or marinade. Pour it over sprouted lentils or raw cruciferous vegetables and let marinate for several hours before serving.

½ cup celery juice

¼ cup raw hemp oil or olive oil

3 tablespoons Nama Shoyu

2 teaspoons mustard seeds

3 garlic cloves, chopped

1 slice fresh ginger

¼ cup agave nectar

Combine the celery juice, oil, Nama Shoyu, mustard seeds, garlic, and ginger in a high-powered blender, and process until smooth. Gradually add the agave nectar to suit your taste.

NOTE: This recipe can be made a day or two before using, if desired.

Teriyaki Sauce .... YIELD: ABOUT ⅔ CUP

⅓ cup Nama Shoyu

2½ teaspoons raw apple cider vinegar

2 tablespoons organic wine, dry sherry, or grape juice (optional)

1½ teaspoons packed rapadura or agave nectar

1½ teaspoons peeled and minced fresh ginger

1 large garlic clove, minced

1 teaspoon raw sesame oil or flaxseed oil

Combine the Nama Shoyu, vinegar, optional wine, rapadura, ginger, and garlic in a high-powered blender, and begin processing. Drizzle in the oil with the machine running. Blend well. Pour into a glass bottle.

Tomato-Free Marinara Sauce

YIELD: 1 CUP

3 beets, peeled and chopped

1½ cups chopped carrots

¼ cup Nama Shoyu

3 tablespoons raw apple cider vinegar

½ onion, chopped

1 tablespoon raw olive oil

2 garlic cloves, minced

½ teaspoon chopped fresh oregano

1 teaspoon Atlantic kelp granules

Combine all the ingredients in a high-powered blender, and process until the desired texture is achieved. Add a few drops of water, if necessary.

Vegan Herb Mayonnaise .... YIELD: 1 CUP

½ cup raw cashews or almonds, soaked

½ cup raw pine nuts, soaked for 30 minutes

1 tablespoon chopped fresh chives

1 tablespoon chopped fresh tarragon

1 tablespoon chopped fresh marjoram (optional)

1 teaspoon chopped fresh parsley

Raw brown mustard seeds, sprouted (optional)

Combine all the ingredients in a high-powered blender, and process until smooth. Add a small amount of water during processing, if necessary. Adjust the seasonings to taste. Use a plunger to keep the mixture moving. Store in an airtight container in the refrigerator.

Watercress Sauce .... YIELD: 2 CUPS

Use this recipe as a salad dressing or a dipping sauce.

1 cup chopped watercress

½ cup Cashew Milk (page 40)

½ cups dry white wine or grape juice (optional)

⅓ cup vegetable broth or carrot juice

1 celery stalk, chopped

2 tablespoons raw olive oil

2 small shallots, chopped

1 teaspoon Celtic sea salt

1 bay leaf, crumbled

Combine all the ingredients in a high-powered blender, and process until smooth.

Winter Holiday Relish .... YIELD: 4 CUPS

Give this as a holiday gift to friends and family.

2 cups cranberries, chopped

2 oranges, peeled and sectioned

1 cup Date Butter (page 152)

½ cup raisins

2 tablespoons grated fresh ginger

2 tablespoons freshly squeezed lime juice

1 teaspoon powdered psyllium husks

Combine the cranberries, oranges, Date Butter, raisins, ginger, and lime juice in a high-powered blender or food processor fitted with the S blade. Gradually add the psyllium powder, and mix thoroughly. Transfer to a Mason jar and seal the lid. Stored in the refrigerator, Winter Holiday Relish will keep for up to 2 weeks.

Allspice

This is easy for children to make, and it is terrific as a gift with a photograph and the name of the child who made it on the container. Keep this seasoning on hand to use in other recipes in this book.

2 tablespoons ground cinnamon

¼ teaspoon ground ginger

¼ teaspoon ground nutmeg

¼ teaspoon ground cloves

¼ teaspoon ground cardamom

¼ teaspoon Ground Lemon Peel (page 169)

Combine all the ingredients in a mortar and use a pestle to pound and mix them. Store in an airtight jar at room temperature.

Ground Lemon Peel

This is handy to use whenever recipes call for lemon zest.

3 to 4 lemons (preferably Meyer lemons)

Peel the skin off the lemons, but do not include the white bitter part. Place it on a dehydrator tray or directly in the sun. If using a dehydrator, turn it to 105 to 108 degrees F. If you are drying it in the sun, please remember to keep moving it as the sun shifts, so it remains in the sun at all times. Once the top is dried, turn it over to dry the other side, and continue drying until it is fully dry and crisp. Wait at least 1 hour, then chop or grind it in a coffee grinder, food processor fitted with the S blade, high-powered blender, or spice mill. Store in an airtight container at room temperature.

Snacks and Desserts

The recipes in this section are short and sweet. Because there is such a wide variety of nutrient-rich, delicious fruits from which to feast, I believe that adding desserts regularly to our diet is redundant. These special treats can be fun to make, however, and I find that this is what brings most people to the raw vegan table. Were it not for the first tastes of the delectable desserts that the raw vegan community excels at making, most people who are now following this diet would never have even considered it! These are the recipes to bring out if family members or visitors scowl when you say you wish to serve them something from your raw vegan kitchen. These recipes are a huge hit at parties and often serve as a gateway to health and healing for those who have been unwilling to change their lifestyles.

Sweet Attack Snack ....

This is a very satisfying, nutritious, and sweet snack that children absolutely love.

3 tablespoons Raw Almond Butter
  (page 160)

1 tablespoon unsweetened shredded
  dried coconut (optional)

Dash of freshly squeezed lemon or
  lime juice

Dash of Celtic sea salt

3 celery stalks

1 tablespoon raisins

Combine the almond butter, optional coconut, lemon juice, and salt in a bowl, and mix until well blended. Line each celery stalk with this mixture, and place the raisins on top.

Sweet Holiday Nuts ....

This is a very popular raw vegan alternative to candy that also makes a great holiday gift.

2 cups raw cashews, soaked

2 cups raw pecans, soaked

2 cups raw walnuts, soaked

2 cups raw almonds, soaked

2 cups raw hazelnuts, soaked

¼ cup agave nectar or yacon syrup

1 tablespoon Allspice (page 169)

¼ teaspoon ground cinnamon

Dash of raw grapeseed oil, olive oil,
  or hemp oil (optional)

Dash of Celtic sea salt

Toss all the ingredients together in a bowl, and let rest for at least 1 hour. Toss again and place on a dehydrator tray, making sure the mixture is spread evenly. Dehydrate at 105 to 108 degrees F for 4 to 5 hours. Turn the nuts over and continue dehydrating until dry and crispy.

Mulberry Candy .... YIELD: 10 TO 12 PIECES

3 tablespoons Raw Almond Butter (page 160)

- 1 cup fresh or dried mulberries (see note)
- 1 tablespoon mesquite powder (optional)
- 1 teaspoon camu camu (optional)

Combine the almond butter and the mulberries in a high-powered blender, and process until smooth. Use a plunger to keep the mixture moving and achieve the proper consistency. Roll the mixture into balls or cut into any desired shape, and refrigerate for 2 to 3 hours before serving. Store leftovers in the refrigerator.

NOTE: If you use dried mulberries, soak them in water or freshly made apple juice for about 1 hour beforehand. Use some of the soaking liquid in the blender for a smoother candy.

Buttered Sticks .... YIELD: 8 TO 10 SERVINGS

Serve these for a quick and satisfying snack or as an hors d'oeuvre at parties.

- 5 or 6 celery stalks
- 4 tablespoons Raw Almond Butter (page 160)
- 4 tablespoons Date Butter (page 152)

Cut the celery stalks in half. Spread the almond butter in the inside groove of half of the celery sticks and the Date Butter in the remainder of the sticks.

Lettuce Snack ....

This is a favorite with children.

2 romaine lettuce leaves

2 tablespoons Raw Almond Butter (page 160)

1 teaspoon agave nectar or chopped dates (optional)

Spread the almond butter in the center of each lettuce leaf. Drizzle on the optional sweetener. Wrap and serve.

NOTE: This is a quick and nutritious way to add greens to your diet while satisfying any desires for sweets that you might still be experiencing.

Seaweed Chips .... YIELD: ABOUT 12 SERVINGS

This is great for traveling or for parties.

6 to 8 raw nori sheets

1 to 2 cups Sunflower Pâté (page 165)

18 cherry tomatoes, thinly sliced

Cut each nori sheet into 16 small squares. Use a spatula or fork to press the pâté onto the nori squares. Put 1 or 2 slices of the cherry tomatoes on top. Dehydrate at 105 to 108 degrees F for 18 to 22 hours.

NOTE: It is beneficial to make a lot of these so you always have some on hand for those days when you are unable to spend time in the kitchen.

Gourmet Flax Veggie Crackers

YIELD: 50 TO 60 CRACKERS

This recipe must be prepared over two or three days before it will be ready to eat. It is a good way to stretch your budget, as these crackers can be enjoyed whenever you don't have time to make something fresh or you are unable to find fresh fruits and vegetables. They are also a gift to yourself and others when you are traveling and have limited access to fresh foods. Top the crackers with any of the spreads in this book to increase your nutritional intake.

2 cups golden or dark flaxseeds

1 cup raw sunflower seeds

1 red bell pepper, coarsely chopped

1 zucchini, coarsely chopped

1 carrot, coarsely chopped

1 onion, coarsely chopped

½ cup chopped fresh parsley

5 to 6 teaspoons freshly squeezed lemon juice

2 garlic cloves

1½ teaspoon Celtic sea salt

Day one: Place the dry flaxseeds in a 4-cup (or larger) container, and fill it to the top with water. Place in a dark spot for 24 hours.

Day two: Soak the sunflower seeds in water for 8 hours. Rinse and drain them. Rinse the soaked flaxseeds well and pour them into a large mixing bowl. Put the sunflower seeds, bell pepper, zucchini, carrot, onion, parsley, lemon juice, garlic, and salt in a food processor fitted with the S blade, and process until well combined and the ingredients are evenly distributed. Be patient, as this may take a while.

Once the ingredients are evenly distributed, place about 3 cups of the mixture on a 16-inch square dehydrator tray covered with a Teflex sheet. Make sure the batter is evenly spread to cover the entire tray. Use a spatula to cut the mixture into 20 to 24 squares before placing it in the dehydrator. Continue this procedure until all of the mixture has been used.

Dehydrate the crackers at 108 degrees F for 1 hour. Turn the temperature down to 105 degrees F and dehydrate for 12 hours longer.

Day three: Flip the trays over and peel off the Teflex sheets. Return the crackers to the dehydrator and continue dehydrating for another 10 to 12 hours

Popsicles ....

These summer coolers are popular with children. Serve them straight from the ice cube tray.

1 Macintosh or Fuji apple

¼ lime

1 tablespoon agave nectar (optional)

Juice the apple and lime. Place the juice in a high-powered blender, and process on low speed. Taste for flavor. If a sweeter taste is desired, add the agave nectar, and process again on low speed. Pour into ice cube trays and freeze. If available, put a Popsicle stick in each ice cube tray before freezing.

Pear Dessert ....

1¼ cups Cashew Milk (page 40)

½ teaspoon vanilla extract

2 Bartlett pears, peeled, cored, and sliced

¼ cup freshly squeezed orange juice

6 tablespoons agave nectar

¼ teaspoon ground cinnamon

¼ teaspoon grated orange peel

Place the milk in a large, flat dish with sides (such as a pie dish). Add the vanilla extract and stir well. Brush the pears with the orange juice. Arrange the pear slices in the dish with the milk. Pour in the agave nectar and mix well. Use a spoon to drizzle the milk over the pears. Sprinkle with the cinnamon and orange peel, and refrigerate for about 2 hours before serving. Serve on individual plates or in dessert bowls, making sure to spoon the milk over the pear slices.

NOTE: For a festive occasion, top this dessert with a spoonful of any of the ice cream recipes in this book.

Applesauce ....

6 to 8 apples

¼ to ½ teaspoon freshly squeezed lemon juice

2 tablespoons water or apple juice

2 tablespoons raw honey or agave nectar, or 2 to 3 pitted honey dates

½ teaspoon ground cinnamon

Dice the apples and sprinkle them with the lemon juice. Place in a high-powered blender with the remaining ingredients, and process on low.

NOTE: If using the dates as a sweetener, more water might be necessary depending on the firmness of the dates.

Cranberry Pear Sauce .... YIELD: ABOUT 4 CUPS

This recipe can be made two or three days in advance.

1 pound Bosc pears

1 orange

½ cup agave nectar

1 star anise, or ¾ teaspoon anise seeds

1 (3-inch long) cinnamon stick

½ cup raw honey

3 cups (about 12 ounces) fresh or frozen cranberries

Peel and core the pears, and cut them into ½-inch cubes. Grate enough of the orange peel (orange part only) to make 1½ teaspoons. Squeeze the juice from the orange; measure, and add enough water to make ½ cup. Pour into a medium mixing bowl, add the grated peel, agave nectar, and star anise, and mix well. Grind the cinnamon stick and add the powder to the juice mixture. Stir in the honey and pears, and mix until thoroughly combined.

Put the cranberries in a food processor fitted with the S blade, and pulse until they are finely chopped. Add the cranberries to the pear mixture and mix well. Serve at room temperature or thoroughly chilled.

Frozen Organic Berries .... YIELD: 5 CUPS

This is prepared in advance for smoothies and ice cream.

1 cup strawberries

1 cup blueberries

1 cup gooseberries

1 cup boysenberries

1 cup blackberries

Place a lint-free towel on a cookie sheet. Rinse the berries thoroughly (swish them in a shallow bowl of water). Allow them to drain for a while. Place the berries on the towel on the cookie sheet (the towel will absorb any excess water). Place the cookie sheet in the freezer until the berries are frozen. When the berries are frozen, lift the towel and the berries will pop off. Store the berries in zipper-lock freezer bags in the freezer.

Chilled Peaches with Raspberries

YIELD: 4 TO 5 SERVINGS

12 freestone peaches

¾ cup freshly squeezed lime juice

½ to ¾ cup agave nectar, Date
    Butter (page 152), or raw honey

2 cups fresh raspberries

4 to 6 peppermint or spearmint
    leaves, for garnish

Cut the peaches in half and remove the stones. Combine the agave nectar and lemon juice and pour over the peach halves. Let rest for 3 to 5 hours in the refrigerator. Transfer to a serving bowl or individual dessert plates or bowls.

Combine 1 cup of the raspberries with some of the mint leaves and a little water in a high-powered blender, and process until smooth. Pour over the peaches. Garnish with the remaining cup of raspberries and mint leaves.

Berry Cheesecake .... Yield: 12 servings

CRUST

2½ cups raw pecans, soaked and dehydrated

¼ cup mesquite powder

¼ cup pitted dates

1 teaspoon grated orange peel

Dash of vanilla extract

FILLING

3 cups raw cashews, soaked 2 hours

1 cup Date Butter (page 152)

1 cup raw coconut oil, liquefied

½ cup freshly squeezed lemon juice

4 tablespoons organic soy lecithin powder (see note)

2 tablespoon vanilla extract

TOPPING

1 pint berries, in season

To make the pie crust, combine the pecans, mesquite powder, dates, orange peel, and vanilla extract in a food processor fitted with the S blade, and process until the mixture begins to stick together. Press evenly into the bottom of an 8-inch springform pan.

To make the filling, place the cashews, Date Butter, and coconut oil in a food processor fitted with the S blade, and process until smooth. This can take up to 10 minutes. Add the lemon juice, soy lecithin powder, and vanilla extract, and process until smooth and creamy. Spread evenly into the prepared pie crust.

Layer the berries over the filling, and press gently until they are slightly embedded. Refrigerate for at least 2 to 3 hours before serving. Store in a covered container in the refrigerator.

NOTE: Check Health Force Nutritionals brand for GMO-free soy lecithin powder.

Citrus Fruit Bowl .... YIELD: 3 TO 4 SERVINGS

½ cup freshly squeezed orange juice

¼ cup raisins or Incan berries (optional)

2 to 3 oranges, peeled and quartered

1 to 2 grapefruits, peeled and quartered

2 to 4 tangerines, peeled and quartered

1 very ripe papaya, peeled, seeded, and cubed

2 to 3 pitted dates, finely chopped

2 tablespoons freshly squeezed lime or lemon juice

4 to 6 peppermint or spearmint leaves, chopped

1 teaspoon lucuma powder

Soak the raisins in the orange juice for 20 to 30 minutes. Place the oranges, grapefruits, tangerines, papaya, dates, and soaked raisins with their soaking liquid in a large glass bowl. Sprinkle with the lemon juice and chill in the refrigerator. Just before serving, add the mint leaves and lucuma powder and stir well.

NOTE: A tasty addition to this fruit bowl is a dollop of Coconut Frosting (page 181) or Date Butter (page 152) just before serving.

Raspberry Parfait .... YIELD: 2 TO 3 SERVINGS

1 pint raspberries

Water, if needed

½ cup pitted honey dates

Mint sprigs, for garnish (optional)

Puree the raspberries in a high-powered blender, gradually adding a small amount of water, if needed. Add the dates, a few at a time, pulsing in between. When all the dates have been added, blend thoroughly until smooth and creamy. Refrigerate until ready to serve. Garnish each serving with a sprig of mint, if desired.

Peaches and Berries .... YIELD: 4 TO 5 SERVINGS

12 freestone peaches

¾ cup freshly squeezed lime juice

¾ cup agave nectar or yacon syrup

2 cups mixed strawberries and raspberries

Cut the peaches in half and remove the stones. Place the peach halves in a mixing bowl. Combine the agave nectar and lime juice (if using agave nectar, only use about ⅓ cup lime juice), and pour over the peaches. Let rest for 2 to 4 hours in the refrigerator.

Drain the liquid from the peaches, and pour it into a high-powered blender. Place the peaches in a serving bowl. Add the strawberries and most of the raspberries to the blender, and process until smooth. Pour over the peaches. Garnish with the remaining raspberries.

Gingerberry Summer Treat

YIELD: 10 TO 12 SERVINGS

This is great for a children's party, or as a refreshing afternoon snack on a hot summer's day.

1 quart blueberries

1 bunch green grapes

1 slice fresh ginger

1 tablespoon agave nectar (optional)

Push the berries and ginger through the hopper of a juicer with the grapes. Stir in the agave nectar, if using. Pour into paper cups. Add wooden Popsicle sticks, and freeze.

NOTE: This can also be made in a high-powered blender, but you will need to add some water to facilitate processing.

Readymade Dessert ....

1 banana, sliced

2 tablespoons Raw Almond Butter (page 160)

1 pitted date, minced

Dash of ground cinnamon

Dash of ground nutmeg

Slice the banana into thin rounds. Place the remaining ingredients in a small bowl, and mix well. Spoon a small amount of this mixture onto each banana round, and serve.

Coconut Frosting ....

This is a great topping for fruit salads and any of the other desserts in this book.
Children love to eat it by itself.

1 orange

2¼ cups Almond Milk (page 34)

2 cups unsweetened shredded dried coconut

½ cup agave nectar

Grate the peel of the orange and set it aside. Juice the orange. Combine the juice and peel with the remaining ingredients in a high-powered blender, and process for 1 to 2 minutes. Spoon a dollop of this frosting on your favorite dessert just before serving.

NOTE: It is best to use this frosting immediately, otherwise the consistency will change.

Mango Pudding .... YIELD: 1 TO 2 SERVINGS

1 cup chopped mangoes

2 tablespoons lucuma powder

1 tablespoon apple juice

1 tablespoon mesquite powder (optional)

Combine all the ingredients in a high-powered blender. Spoon the pudding into individual dessert bowls. Chill thoroughly before serving.

Coconut Custard .... YIELD: 3 SERVINGS

2 cups young Thai coconut flesh

4 to 6 tablespoons raw agave nectar

2 to 3 tablespoons Raw Almond Butter (page 160)

1 tablespoon lucuma powder

1 tablespoon raw coconut oil (optional)

Coconut water, if needed

Combine all the ingredients in a high-powered blender, and process until smooth and creamy. Add a small amount of coconut water, if necessary, to facilitate blending. Use a plunger to keep the mixture moving. Serve at once or thoroughly chilled.

Lemony Custard .... YIELD: 3 TO 4 SERVINGS

5 tablespoons freshly squeezed lemon juice

1 banana, sliced

2 cups coconut flesh

1 cup coconut water

8 to 10 pitted dates, soaked

1 tablespoon agave nectar or raw honey

1 vanilla bean, scraped, or 1 tablespoon vanilla extract

1 teaspoon slippery elm powder (use only if agar flakes are being used)

Dash of rose hips water

2 tablespoons psyllium husk powder or agar flakes

3 to 4 strawberries, sliced, for garnish

Toss the banana with the lemon juice, and set aside to soak. Combine the coconut flesh, coconut water, dates, agave nectar, vanilla bean pulp, agar flakes (if using), slippery elm powder (if using), and rose hips water in a high-powered blender, and process until smooth. Adjust the sweetness to taste. If using psyllium, add it gradually in small amounts at the very end of blending.

Pour the pudding into individual serving bowls, and chill in the refrigerator for 3 to 4 hours. Just before serving, garnish with the strawberries and bananas.

Fun Pear Salad .... YIELD: 2 SERVINGS

1 medium pear, cored and cut into 1-inch chunks

1 medium orange, peeled, quartered, and sliced

¼ cup freshly squeezed orange juice

Combine the pear, orange slices, and orange juice in a small bowl and mix well. Refrigerate for 1 hour before serving.

Tantalizing Chocolate Banana Pudding

YIELD: 2 TO 3 SERVINGS

This recipe is jam-packed with chlorophyll and is a favorite with chocolate lovers.

1 ripe avocado

1 banana

¼ cup raw cacao powder

4 pitted dates, soaked for about 1 hour

1 tablespoon E3Live

1 tablespoon lucuma powder

Dash of ground cinnamon

Dash of salt

Combine all the ingredients in a high-powered blender on low speed until it is smooth and the consistency of pudding. Chill thoroughly before serving.

VARIATION: If you prefer, substitute an equal amount of raw carob powder for the cacao powder.

Cherimoya Pudding .... YIELD: 1 TO 2 SERVINGS

1 cup chopped cherimoya flesh

1 tablespoon lucuma powder

1 teaspoon mesquite powder (optional)

1 sapote, cut into small round pieces and frozen

Combine the cherimoya, lucuma powder, and mesquite powder in a high-powered blender. Transfer to dessert bowls, and mix in pieces of the frozen sapote just before serving.

Holiday Pumpkin Spice Pudding

2 cups peeled and coarsely chopped pumpkin or winter squash

1 cup Almond Milk (page 34) or Cashew Milk (page 40)

½ cup currants, soaked

3 to 5 tablespoons raw honey or agave nectar

1 tablespoon raw coconut oil

1 tablespoon raw tahini

1 tablespoon agar flakes

1 tablespoon Raw Almond Butter (page 160)

1½ teaspoons pumpkin pie spice or Allspice (page 169)

1 teaspoon slippery elm powder

Combine all the ingredients in a high-powered blender, and process for 1 to 2 minutes until creamy. Pour into desserts bowls or glasses. Serve thoroughly chilled.

VARIATION: This pudding may also be used as a filling for Pie Crust (page 193). Chill the pie thoroughly before serving.

NOTE: If you are short on time and unable to make fresh almond butter, use raw almond butter from a jar.

Durian Ice Cream.................... YIELD: 2 TO 3 SERVINGS

1 cup chopped untreated durian

1 cup soft raw hempseeds

½ cup Cashew Milk (page 40)

6 to 8 pitted dates

1 tablespoon agave nectar

1 teaspoon freshly squeezed lime juice

Combine all the ingredients in a high-powered blender, and freeze for 1 to 2 hours before serving.

NOTE: If you do not freeze this recipe, it can be served as a pudding.

Banana Ice Cream .... YIELD: 2 TO 3 SERVINGS

The addition of the camu camu gives this delightful dessert a powerful boost of vitamin C.

2 to 4 frozen bananas

1 cup frozen raw almonds (soaked and dehydrated before freezing)

1 tablespoon lucuma powder

1 teaspoon camu camu powder (optional)

1 drop vanilla extract (optional)

Alternate putting the bananas and almonds through the hopper of a juicer using the blank screen. Alternatively, process them in a high-powered blender, and use a plunger to keep the mixture moving. Add the lucuma powder and optional camu camu powder; then add a drop of vanilla extract, if desired. Stir well. Serve immediately in chilled dessert dishes.

NOTE: This ice cream will melt if it is not consumed immediately or stored in the freezer.

Strawberry Ice Cream .... <small>YIELD: 3 TO 4 SERVINGS</small>

This is a favorite at parties on hot summer days.

1 cup frozen strawberries

2 frozen bananas

3 to 5 tablespoons apple juice, if needed

Combine the strawberries and bananas in a high-powered blender, and process until smooth. Add a small amount of apple juice, if necessary, to facilitate blending. Use a plunger to keep the mixture moving. Serve immediately in chilled dessert bowls.

NOTE: If you prefer, you can process the strawberries and bananas through the hopper of a juicer using the blank screen. You will not need to use any apple juice.

Nutty Ice Cream .... <small>YIELD: 4 TO 5 SERVINGS</small>

1 cup frozen raw almonds (soaked and dehydrated before freezing)

2 very ripe frozen bananas

2 tablespoons raw pistachios

Alternate putting the almonds, bananas, and pistachios through the hopper of a juicer using the blank screen. Place a chilled bowl under the spout to catch the ice cream and keep it from melting. Serve immediately in chilled dessert bowls.

NOTE: Always have a stash of almonds in the freezer that have been soaked and then dehydrated so you can quickly make ice cream and other recipes that call for frozen almonds.

Tutti-Frutti Ice Cream .... YIELD : ABOUT 4 SERVINGS

This is a quick recipe that is a favorite at birthday parties and other festive gatherings. Your guests won't believe it doesn't contain any milk or sugar!

2 frozen bananas

½ cup frozen chopped pineapple

1 apple, shredded and sprinkled with freshly squeezed lime juice

1 handful pitted fresh cherries, chopped

3 to 6 raisins or mulberries

Unsweetened dried coconut flakes, for garnish

Combine the bananas, pineapple, and apple in a high-powered blender, and process until smooth. Use a plunger to keep the mixture moving. Transfer to chilled dessert bowls, and place the cherries and raisins on the top and sides. Sprinkle with the coconut flakes, and serve immediately.

Carob Ice Cream .... YIELD: 2 SERVINGS

2 frozen bananas

2 to 3 dried figs (soaked for 20 minutes; keep the soaking water in case it is needed)

1 tablespoon raw carob powder

1 tablespoon dried mulberries

1 tablespoon lucuma powder

Combine all the ingredients in a high-powered blender, gradually adding some of the fig soak water, if necessary, to facilitate blending and achieve a smooth consistency. Serve immediately in chilled dessert bowls.

Coconut Ice Cream .... YIELD: 4 SERVINGS

- 1 cup frozen coconut flesh
- 2 frozen bananas
- 2 to 3 pitted dates, chopped
- Coconut water, if needed

Combine all the ingredients in a high-powered blender. Add a very small amount of coconut water, if necessary, to facilitate blending, and process until smooth. Use a plunger to keep the mixture moving. If you prefer to use a juicer with a blank screen, alternate the ingredients as you push them through the hopper. Place a chilled bowl under the spout of the juicer to catch the ice cream and keep it from melting. Serve immediately in chilled dessert bowls.

Mango Berry Ice Cream .... YIELD: 3 TO 4 SERVINGS

- 2 frozen bananas
- 3 to 6 tablespoons frozen chopped strawberries
- 2 mangoes, peeled and chopped

Alternate the bananas and strawberries through the hopper of a juicer with the blank screen in place. Place a chilled bowl under the spout of the juicer to catch the ice cream and keep it from melting. Stir in the chopped mangoes. Serve immediately in chilled dessert bowls.

Peaches and Coconut Ice Cream

YIELD: 4 TO 5 SERVINGS

1 coconut

1 cup frozen peaches

1 cup ice (optional)

2 frozen bananas

½ cup raw macadamia nuts (optional)

4 to 5 pitted dates

1 tablespoon agave nectar (optional)

1 tablespoon lucuma powder (optional)

1 tablespoon apple juice, if needed

1 teaspoon raw flaxseed oil or walnut oil (optional)

Open the coconut. Pour the coconut water into a high-powered blender. Scoop out the coconut flesh and add it to the blender along with the remaining ingredients. Process on high speed, adding a small amount of the apple juice, only if needed, to facilitate processing and achieve the proper consistency. Use a plunger to keep the mixture moving. Serve immediately in chilled dessert bowls, or pour into ice cube trays and freeze.

Peaches and Cream .... YIELD: 2 TO 3 SERVINGS

1 coconut

2 peaches, sliced and frozen

1 frozen banana

½ cup frozen raw cashews or macadamia nuts

2 to 3 pitted dates, frozen

Open the coconut and pour the water into a bowl. Scoop out the flesh and place it in a high-powered blender. Add the remaining ingredients, and process until smooth. Use a plunger to keep the mixture moving. Add a small amount of the coconut water, if necessary, to facilitate blending and achieve the desired consistency. Alternatively, alternate putting the coconut flesh, peaches, banana, cashews, and dates through the hopper of a juicer using the blank screen. Place a chilled bowl under the spout to catch the ice cream and keep it from melting. Serve immediately in chilled dessert bowls or wine glasses.

Cherry Vanilla Almond Ice Cream

YIELD: ABOUT 6 SERVINGS

2 cups Almond Milk (page 34)

2 cups raw cashews, soaked for 4 hours, rinsed, and drained

2 pints frozen pitted cherries

1 cup agave nectar

2¼ teaspoons psyllium powder

1½ teaspoons vanilla extract

1 vanilla bean, scraped

Dash of Celtic sea salt

3 to 4 pitted fresh cherries, chopped

Combine the Almond Milk, cashews, frozen cherries, agave nectar, psyllium powder, vanilla extract, vanilla bean pulp, and salt in a high-powered blender, and process until smooth and creamy.

Pour into a 9-inch square glass baking dish or other shallow glass container, and cover tightly. Freeze for 10 to 12 hours, or until the ice cream is firm. Serve immediately in chilled dessert bowls, and sprinkle with the fresh cherries. Alternatively, store in an airtight container in the freezer, and sprinkle with the fresh cherries just before serving.

L'shanah Tovah Honey Cake

This is the raw version of the traditional sweet cake served on the Jewish New Year.

3½ cups raw almond meal or almond pulp (from making Almond Milk, page 34)

1 cup mesquite powder

1 cup raw honey

¼ cup yacon syrup or Date Butter (page 152)

2 to 4 tablespoons raw coconut oil

1 tablespoon vanilla extract

1½ teaspoons agar flakes or slippery elm powder

½ teaspoon ground cinnamon

¼ teaspoon ground cloves

¼ teaspoon grated orange peel

Dash of Celtic sea salt

1 cup grated apples

½ cup raw pecans

Combine the almond meal, mesquite powder, honey, yacon syrup, coconut oil, vanilla extract, agar flakes, cinnamon, cloves, orange peel, and salt in a food processor fitted with the S blade, and process until well blended. Transfer to a cake pan or loaf pan, add the apples and pecans, and mix well. Flatten the top, cover, and refrigerate for a few hours before serving. Alternatively, the cake may be dehydrated at 105 to 108 degrees F for 2 to 3 hours. Remove it from the pan, turn it over, and continue to dehydrate until the desired texture is achieved. Serve immediately or store it in the refrigerator.

NOTES: This is a great opportunity to use the almond pulp that is left over when you make Almond Milk (page 34). Be careful not to add too much pulp to the recipe, however, as that can make it too heavy.

• Should you decide to dehydrate the mixture, the resulting texture will be more like a cake, but it will be drier. You might even wish to dehydrate it for a longer period so it will store better and look even more like a conventional cake.

Mud Pie ....

This is a very handy and quick recipe when you want something sweet and satisfying.

1 cup Raw Almond Butter (page 160)

2 ripe bananas, sliced

2 to 3 pitted dates, minced

¼ teaspoon ground cinnamon

¼ teaspoon ground nutmeg

1½ teaspoons unsweetened dried coconut flakes (optional)

Combine the almond butter, bananas, dates, cinnamon, and nutmeg in a bowl, and mix well. Top with the optional coconut flakes. Eat as is, or roll into balls to make candy.

Pie Crust ....

This pie crust can be used for both savory and sweet dishes.

1 cup ground soaked and dehydrated raw almonds

½ cup ground soaked and dehydrated raw hazelnuts

2 to 4 pitted dates

1 tablespoon raw coconut oil (optional)

2 teaspoons raw honey or agave nectar

½ teaspoon ground cinnamon

Dash of Celtic sea salt

Combine all the ingredients in a food processor fitted with the S blade, and process into a dough. Transfer to a pie plate. Flatten the mixture with your fingers (use food-handling gloves) to fill the entire plate. Use immediately or store in the freezer.

Velvety Vegan Pumpkin Pie

YIELD: 6 TO 8 SERVINGS

This is a holiday favorite.

1½ cups coconut flesh (reserve water)

2 cups raw pumpkin pulp (blended in a food processor)

¾ cup stevia powder or liquid or agave nectar

1 teaspoon vanilla extract

1½ teaspoons ground cinnamon

¾ teaspoon ground ginger

¼ teaspoon ground nutmeg

⅛ teaspoon ground cloves

Dash of Allspice (page 169)

1 Pie Crust (page 193)

Put the coconut flesh along with some of the reserved coconut water in a high-powered blender or food processor fitted with the S blade, and process on high speed until smooth. Add the pumpkin pulp, stevia, vanilla extract, cinnamon, ginger, nutmeg, cloves, and Allspice, and mix well. Pour the mixture into the pie crust and freeze for 2 to 3 hours. If the filling seems too soft after blending, place it in the refrigerator to chill before pouring it into the piecrust. Serve frozen.

NOTE: Always return any unused portion to the freezer immediately after serving this pie.

Coconut Chewies ....

The addition of E3Live enhances the nutritional content of this recipe and is a unique way to add valuable greens to the diet.

3 cups unsweetened shredded dried coconut

1 cup raw macadamia nuts or cashews, soaked

½ lemon, peeled and seeded

3 to 4 tablespoons agave nectar

1 ounce E3Live, thawed, or E3AFA dried flakes (optional)

1 teaspoon ground cinnamon

Dash of ground cardamom

Dash of vanilla extract

Place the coconut in a medium mixing bowl and set aside. Place the nuts in a high-powered blender and cover with water for 1 hour. Do not remove the water. When the hour is up, add the lemon to the blender, and process on high speed until thick and creamy. Add more water, if necessary, to facilitate blending. If using E3Live liquid, add it now. Add the agave nectar to taste and blend again. Then add the cinnamon, cardamom, and vanilla extract to taste. Pour over the coconut and mix well.

Drop a spoonful at a time onto a dehydrator tray with a Teflex sheet. If using the E3AFA dried flakes, place a generous amount on top of each cookie. Dehydrate the cookies at 105 degrees F until they are dry to the touch. Flip them over and continue to dehydrate until they are thoroughly dried all the way through.

Liquid Meals

I am often asked about the need for supplements. This chapter is my answer to that. If your diet needs supplementation, it is likely due to one or more of the following:

- Your body is not being supported with the nutrients, air, and water it needs to regularly detoxify, rebuild, and do its constant job of maintenance.
- You are a professional athlete, training long, arduous hours with not much time to devote to adequate rest, and you feel depleted.
- You are a triathlete undertaking a demanding training schedule and need a high-energy, nutrient-dense diet. You may also need an easy-to-consume source of carbohydrates that minimizes the risk of gastrointestinal upset.
- You are menstruating or pregnant.

- You are recovering from a debilitating illness and the process of digestion takes too much energy away from your healing.
- You have chronic digestive disorders.
- You have a fractured jaw or have had extensive dental work done and do not wish to consider fasting.
- You wish to "go raw" but you are having problems digesting raw vegetables, nuts, and grains, and find yourself eating an overabundance of fruits.
- You have days when you just do not have the time to sit and eat mindfully.
- You are traveling and are unsure of the food supply during your journey. You might wish to make some of these recipes and pack them in airtight containers. If necessary, you can freeze a few beforehand (though this might diminish the enzyme content a bit).

Liquid meals are also helpful when time is at a premium. Use them occasionally to supplement your usual food intake, not replace it. If you dine on liquid meals exclusively, you will be missing out on important fiber.

I have included E3Live in some of these recipes (as well as in other sections of this book) because I see it as a very concentrated food source that has tremendous value. It ensures that we have a full range of nutrients available in a very convenient form.

Mint Julep .... Yield: 2 servings

2 Granny Smith apples

1 to 2 celery stalks

1 small cucumber

1 handful fresh mint

2 to 3 pitted dates

Push the apples, celery, cucumber, and mint though the hopper of a juicer. Pour into a high-powered blender, and add the dates. Process until completely smooth. Chill thoroughly before serving.

Avocado Drink .... Yield: 2 servings

1 ripe avocado

1 cup carrot juice

1 cup coarsely chopped cucumbers

1 handful fresh dill

Dash of freshly squeezed lemon juice

Dash of Celtic sea salt

Combine all the ingredients in a high-powered blender. Adjust lemon juice and salt to taste.

Carrot Avocado Medley .... Yield: 4 servings

2 cups carrot juice

1 very ripe avocado

1 cup celery juice

1 tomato, quartered

1 rose geranium leaf or dash of rose water (optional)

Fresh dill, to taste

Dash of Celtic sea salt

Dash of cayenne

Combine all the ingredients in a high-powered blender, and process until smooth. Adjust the seasonings to taste.

Spicy Broccoli in a Glass ...... YIELD: 1 TO 2 SERVINGS

3 broccoli florets

2 carrots

1 tomato

1 garlic clove

2 celery stalks

1 bell pepper

1 teaspoon Sambal Olek (page 154),
    more or less to taste

Use the broccoli and carrots to push the tomato and garlic through the hopper of a juicer Follow with the celery and bell pepper. Pour into a high-powered blender, adding the Sambal Olek gradually, adjusting the amount to your taste. Process until well combined, and pour into serving glasses.

NOTE: For a milder version, omit the Sambal Olek.

Carrot Delight .... YIELD: 3 CUPS

This is a great breakfast choice during holidays and other festive occasions. When you are feeling tempted to succumb to the social pressure for cooked foods, drink this and you will be reminded of the pleasures offered by raw vegan cuisine.

2 cups carrot juice

1 cup Macadamia Nut Milk (page 34)
    or Cashew Milk (page 40)

1 slice fresh ginger

1 vanilla bean, scraped

1 cardamom seed

Dash of ground nutmeg

Dash of ground cinnamon

1 to 2 pitted dates, or 1 teaspoon
    agave nectar (optional)

Combine the carrot juice, nut milk, ginger, vanilla bean pulp, cardamom, nutmeg, and cinnamon in a high-powered blender, and process until smooth and creamy. Add the dates if you prefer a sweeter taste. Chill thoroughly before serving.

Carrot Ginger Drink .... YIELD: 2 SERVINGS

1 cup carrot juice

½ cup Almond Milk (page 34) or Cashew Milk (page 40)

1 tablespoon raw flaxseed oil or hemp oil

1 teaspoon yacon syrup or agave nectar (optional)

1 teaspoon minced fresh ginger

¼ teaspoon ground cinnamon

Combine all the ingredients in a high-powered blender, and process until smooth and creamy.

Chlorophyll Cocktail .... YIELD: 2 SERVINGS

This will fortify you all day long whenever you are unable to sit down for a meal. Just remember to drink lots of water throughout the day.

3 beet tops

1 handful fresh parsley

1 handful spinach

4 carrots

1 apple

1 to 2 tablespoons E3Live

⅛ teaspoon Ultimate Mega H
(see note)

Bunch up the beet tops, parsley, and spinach and push through hopper of a juicer with the carrots and apple. Pour into a serving glass. Add the E3Live and Ultimate Mega H, and mix well. Drink immediately.

NOTE: Ultimate Mega H is the brand name for a product that contains a naturally occurring hydrogen energy ion that supports your body's ability to eliminate free radicals. Hydrogen is a powerful antioxidant that helps keep your cells hydrated. It works synergistically with E3Live to provide enhanced health benefits.

Clean Green Soup .... YIELD: 2 SERVINGS

2 green apples

1 small, ripe avocado

1 handful sunflower sprouts

¼ cup raw dulse

1 celery stalk

Dash of cayenne

Combine all the ingredients in a high-powered blender, and process until smooth. Add just enough water to facilitate blending and achieve the desired consistency. Pour into glasses or bowls and serve.

NOTE: If you prefer, juice the apples, sprouts, and celery in a masticating juicer; then transfer the juice to a high-powered blender. This will produce a clearer and more fluid meal, although it will contain less fiber. This may be a preferable method if you are recovering from an illness or surgery.

Cleansing Cocktail .... YIELD: 2 SERVINGS

Be sure to drink this slowly and mindfully.

4 carrots

1 beet

1 apple

1 (¼-inch) piece fresh ginger

Use the carrots to push the other ingredients through the hopper of a juicer.

Alkaline Enhancer .... YIELD: 3 TO 4 SERVINGS

1 to 2 Granny Smith apples

3 celery stalks

¼ head cabbage

Push all the ingredients through the hopper of a juicer. Alternatively, coarsely chop all the ingredients, and place them in a high-powered blender. Add a small amount of water to facilitate blending, and process until completely smooth. If desired, strain before serving.

Coconut Carrot Drink .... YIELD: 2 SERVINGS

Use this recipe for a boost of quick, sustained energy.

4 to 5 carrots

1 young Thai coconut, water and flesh

Juice the carrots, and pour the juice in a high-powered blender. Crack open the coconut. Pour the coconut water into the blender. Scoop out the flesh, and add it to the blender. Process until smooth. Serve chilled, if desired.

Coconut Smoothie .... YIELD: 4 SERVINGS

1 young Thai coconut, water and flesh

2 cups chopped pineapple

1 cup raw cashews or macadamia nuts

1 cup water

1 fresh or frozen banana

1 Red Delicious apple, peeled and coarsely chopped

½ lemon, juiced

1 tablespoon raw coconut oil, flaxseed oil, or grapeseed oil

Pour the coconut water into a high-powered blender. Scoop out the flesh, and add it to the blender along with the remaining ingredients. Process until smooth and creamy. If necessary, add a little water to facilitate blending and achieve the desired consistency. Chill thoroughly before serving.

NOTE: If you have Cashew Milk (page 40) or Macadamia Nut Milk (page 34) already made, you can use that in lieu of the nuts and water.

Collard Greens in a Glass .... Yield: 2 servings

- 1 Granny Smith apple
- 2 collard leaves
- 2 celery stalks
- 1 to 2 garlic cloves
- 1 tomato
- Dash of Celtic sea salt

Push the apple, collard leaves, celery, and garlic through the hopper of a juicer. Pour into a high-powered blender, and add the tomato and salt to taste. Process until smooth.

NOTE: To retain the fiber of the fruits and vegetables, instead of using a juicer, combine all the ingredients in a high-powered blender, and process until smooth. Add a small amount of water, if necessary, to facilitate blending and achieve the desired consistency.

Colon Mover .... Yield: 2 servings

Drink this first thing in the morning.

- 4 to 5 carrots
- 1 bunch spinach

Use the carrots to push the spinach through the hopper of a juicer.

NOTE: To retain the fiber of the vegetables, instead of using a juicer, chop the carrots and spinach and place them in a high-powered blender. Add 2 cups of water, and process until smooth. If necessary, add a small amount of additional water to facilitate blending and achieve the desired consistency.

Garden Cocktail ....

Chili oil gives this drink a spicy kick. For a milder cocktail, use olive oil.

1 carrot

1 red bell pepper

1 cup chopped lettuce

1 to 2 beefsteak tomatoes

1 parsley sprig

½ teaspoon raw chili oil or olive oil

Dash of cayenne

Dash of Celtic sea salt

Push the vegetables and parsley through the hopper of a juicer, using the carrot to push the tomatoes through. Add the oil and salt to taste. Stir well. Alternatively, chop the vegetables, combine all the ingredients in a high-powered blender, and process on high speed, adding water as necessary to facilitate blending and achieve the desired consistency. Chill thoroughly before serving.

Heavenly Carrot Juice .... YIELD: 2 TO 3 SERVINGS

1 young Thai coconut, water and flesh

5 to 6 carrots, juiced

½ cup Macadamia Nut Milk (page 34)

1 mint sprig

Pour the coconut water into a high-powered blender. Add the carrot juice, nut milk, and mint. Scoop out the coconut flesh and add it to the blender. Process until smooth. Serve at once or thoroughly chilled. To serve, pour into wine glasses or champagne flutes.

Cucumber Cooler .... YIELD: 3 SERVINGS

3 to 4 cucumbers

2 celery stalks

Dash of Flower of the Ocean sea minerals

Push the cucumber and celery through the hopper of a juicer. Pour into serving glasses. Add the sea minerals to taste. Chill thoroughly before serving.

Green Monster ....

This drink is rich in folic acid.

2 carrots

1 cup spinach

1 cup coarsely chopped cabbage

1 bunch beet greens

1 to 2 kale leaves

1 tablespoon freshly squeezed lemon juice

1 garlic clove

1 teaspoon Nama Shoyu

Dash of cayenne (optional)

Push the carrots, spinach, cabbage, beet greens, and kale through the hopper of a juicer. Transfer to a high-powered blender, add the remaining ingredients, and process until smooth.

NOTE: To retain the fiber of the vegetables, instead of using a juicer, chop the carrots and leafy greens and place them in a high-powered blender with the cabbage. Add 2 cups of water and the remaining ingredients, and process until smooth. If necessary, add a small amount of additional water to facilitate blending and achieve the desired consistency.

Creamy Carrot Soup .... YIELD: 4 TO 5 SERVINGS

4 to 5 carrots

2 to 3 cups water

¾ cup raw almonds, soaked

½ teaspoon ground cardamom

1 slice fresh ginger

Dash of Celtic sea salt

Juice the carrots. Transfer the juice to a high-powered blender, and add the remaining ingredients. Process until smooth and creamy.

NOTE: To retain the fiber of the ingredients, instead of using a juicer, chop the carrots and combine them with the remaining ingredients in a high-powered blender. Process until smooth and creamy. Adjust the amount of water to achieve the desired consistency

Green Smoothie #1 .... YIELD: 3 TO 4 SERVINGS

Drink mindfully and with gratitude.

3 Granny Smith apples, quartered

2 watercress sprigs

4 kiwis, peeled

1 to 2 cups apple juice

Combine all the ingredients in a high-powered blender, and process until smooth. Serve in tall glasses.

Green Smoothie #2 .... YIELD: 1 SERVING

1 large pineapple

⅔ cup blueberries

20 watercress sprigs, plus 1 for garnish

Cut the pineapple and push it through the hopper of a juicer. Pour the juice into a high-powered blender, and add the blueberries and watercress. Process until smooth. Chill before serving, if desired. Serve with a sprig of watercress on top.

NOTE: Alternatively, peel and chop the pineapple, and place it in a high-powered blender along with the blueberries and watercress. Add a small amount of water, as needed, to facilitate blending and achieve the desired consistency.

Hair Tonic .... YIELD: 2 TO 3 SERVINGS

3 carrots

1 bunch spinach

3 lettuce leaves

1 tablespoon E3Live

⅛ teaspoon Ultimate Mega H (see page 200)

Push the spinach and lettuce through the hopper of a juicer with the carrots. Pour the juice into a glass. Add the E3Live and Ultimate Mega H, stir well, and drink immediately.

Herbed Tomato Soup ....

2 to 4 cups water

2 cups chopped tomatoes

1 cup sun-dried tomatoes, soaked and chopped

1 mint sprig

½ teaspoon chopped fresh basil

½ teaspoon chopped fresh oregano

Dash of Celtic sea salt

Combine all the ingredients in a high-powered blender, and process until smooth. Adjust the amount of water to achieve the desired consistency. Serve at once or thoroughly chilled.

Herb Tonic .... YIELD: 2 SERVINGS

4 carrots

2 celery stalks

1 handful fresh parsley

1 handful fresh cilantro

1 cilantro sprig

1 mint sprig

1 garlic clove

¼ teaspoon chopped fresh sorrel

Push all of the ingredients through the hopper of a juicer using the carrots and celery. Serve in wine glasses or champagne flutes.

VARIATION: To make a soup, chop all the ingredients and process them in a high-powered blender along with enough water to create a soupy consistency. Pour into a soup bowl, and add a dash of Celtic sea salt or Nama Shoyu to taste.

Liquid Cabbage .... YIELD: 1 SERVING

Many people have found this beverage to be a great way to calm ulcers.

3 celery stalks

¼ head purple cabbage

1 apple, quartered

Push all the ingredients through the hopper of a juicer. Drink immediately.

NOTE: To be effective, cabbage juice must be consumed immediately after it has been made

Liquid Kale .... YIELD: 2 SERVINGS

3 to 4 kale leaves

3 to 4 carrots

1 apple, quartered

1 handful fresh parsley

Push everything through the hopper of a juicer with the carrots, and serve in tall glasses.

Liquid Lettuce .... YIELD: 1 SERVING

5 to 6 lettuce leaves

2 carrots

1 celery stalk

1 apple, quartered

Bunch up the lettuce and push it through the hopper of a juicer with the carrots, celery, and apple. Serve immediately.

NOTE: To retain the fiber in the lettuce, juice only the carrots, celery, and apples. Place the juice along with the lettuce in a high-powered blender, and process until the desired consistency is achieved.

Liquid Salad ....

1 cucumber

1 Granny Smith apple, quartered

1 handful spinach

2 tomatoes

1 kale leaf

1 turnip leaf

1 garlic clove

1 tablespoon freshly squeezed lemon juice

Dash of Flower of the Ocean sea minerals (optional)

Dash of cayenne

Use the cucumber and apple to push the vegetables and garlic through the hopper of a juicer. Add the lemon juice. Season with the sea minerals and cayenne to taste.

Midmorning Cocktail .... YIELD: 1 TO 2 SERVINGS

This drink is highly recommended for those with digestive disorders and to assist in bringing nourishment to the body at peak periods of the day.

1 slice fresh ginger

1 to 2 peppermint leaves

4 carrots

1 apple

Push the peppermint though the hopper of a juicer by wrapping it around the ginger. Make sure to use only a small amount of ginger. Push the apples and carrots (alternating them) through the hopper. Pour into a glass and serve.

NOTE: This can be served as a digestive about 30 minutes before a dinner party.

Midmorning Booster .... YIELD: 2 TO 3 SERVINGS

2 bananas, broken in half

1 carrot, chopped

1 orange, peeled

1 apple, peeled and coarsely chopped

1 mango, peeled and sliced

½ cup Almond Milk (page 34)

1 lemon, juiced

1½ teaspoons raw olive oil (optional)

½ teaspoon ground cinnamon

Water, as needed

Combine all the ingredients in a high-powered blender, adding a small amount of water, if needed, to facilitate blending and achieve the desired consistency. Process until smooth.

Mineral Tonic........................ YIELD: 2 TO 3 SERVINGS

1 handful fresh parsley

2 turnip leaves

1 kale leaf

4 to 5 carrots

1 tablespoon E3Live

⅛ teaspoon Ultimate Mega H (see page 200)

Roll up the parley, turnip leaves, and kale leaf, and push them through the hopper of a juicer with the carrots. Pour into a glass. Add the E3Live and Ultimate Mega H, and mix well. Drink immediately.

Minty Tomato Juice

4 to 6 large, very ripe tomatoes

1 to 2 cups water

1 handful fresh mint

Dash of freshly squeezed lemon juice

Dash of Celtic sea salt (optional)

Combine all the ingredients in a high-powered blender, using just enough of the water to facilitate blending and achieve the desired consistency. Chill thoroughly before serving.

Pineapple High-Protein Shake

YIELD: 2 SERVINGS

½ large pineapple (do not peel)

½ cup Almond Milk (page 34)

1 frozen ripe banana

3 to 4 pitted dates (optional)

2 to 3 tablespoons raw hempseed powder

1 teaspoon raw hemp oil (optional)

Juice the pineapple. Pour the juice into a high-powered blender. Add the remaining ingredients, and process until smooth.

Natural Laxative

YIELD: 1 SERVING

Drink this beverage by itself.

2 apples, quartered

1 pear, quartered

1 cup water

2 to 3 pitted prunes

Combine all the ingredients in a high-powered blender, and process until smooth.

Potassium Broth ....

1 bunch spinach

1 bunch fresh parsley

4 to 5 carrots

2 celery stalks

1 teaspoon freshly squeezed lemon
    juice (optional)

1 teaspoon Nama Shoyu

Push the parsley and spinach through the hopper of a juicer with the carrots and celery, alternating them. Pour into a glass and add the Nama Shoyu and lemon juice.

NOTE: Alternatively, chop the vegetables and place them in a high-powered blender. Add 1 to 2 cups of water (or more, if needed) to facilitate blending and achieve the desired consistency. Process on high speed until smooth. Season with the optional lemon juice and Nama Shoyu to taste, and mix well.

Green Surprise ....

1 large kale leaf

2 to 3 green apples, quartered

1 lime wedge

Bunch up the kale leaf and push it through hopper of a juicer with the apples. Pour the juice into a glass and squeeze in the lime juice. Mix and serve.

NOTE: Alternatively, chop the kale leaf and apples and place in a high-powered blender. Add the juice from the lime wedge and 1 to 2 cups of water. Process at high speed until the desired consistency is achieved. Drink immediately.

Creamy High-Protein Drink ...... YIELD: 2 CUPS

1 cup Almond Milk (page 34)

1 small, ripe avocado

½ cup raw dulse, soaked

¼ cup beet juice

1 tablespoon raw hempseeds

1 tablespoon Incan berries

1 teaspoon raw hemp oil (optional)

1 teaspoon agave nectar or yacon syrup (optional)

1 teaspoon mesquite powder

Combine all the ingredients in a high-powered blender, and process until smooth and creamy. Serve in a tall glass.

Super Protein Booster .... YIELD: 2 CUPS

1 cup Almond Milk (page 34)

1 cup Sesame Milk (page 53)

1 banana

6 to 8 pitted dates

1 tablespoon hempseed powder

1 tablespoon maca powder

1 tablespoon Incan berries

1 tablespoon E3Live

1 teaspoon raw black sesame seeds or raw sesame butter

⅛ teaspoon Ultimate Mega H (see page 200)

Dash of ground cinnamon

Dash of ground cardamom

Dash of ground nutmeg

Combine all the ingredients in a high-powered blender, and process until smooth and creamy. Serve immediately.

Quick and Easy Borscht .... YIELD: 1 SERVING

½ cup carrot juice

¼ cup beet juice

¼ cup cucumber juice

1 tablespoon umeboshi vinegar

1 teaspoon freshly squeezed lemon juice

½ teaspoon Celtic sea salt

1 garlic clove

Pour the freshly made juices into a high-powered blender, and add the remaining ingredients. Process until smooth and well blended.

Quick Fortifier .... YIELD: 1 SERVING

Drink this if you are feeling weak and drained, or simply to stay nutritionally balanced.

1 cup carrot juice

1 tablespoon E3Live

⅛ teaspoon Ultimate Mega H (see page 200)

Combine all the ingredients in a glass, stir well, and drink immediately but slowly.

Spicy Tomato Cocktail .... YIELD: 2 SERVINGS

3 to 4 very ripe heirloom tomatoes

2 celery stalks

¼ teaspoon Jamaican red pepper sauce or Sambal Olek (page 154)

¼ teaspoon Flower of the Ocean sea minerals

Dash of ground cumin

Combine all the ingredients in a high-powered blender, and process on low speed. Add water, if necessary, to achieve the desired consistency.

Green Broth ....

1 handful spinach

1 handful fresh cilantro

1 handful fresh parsley

4 to 5 carrots

1 green apple, quartered

2 celery stalks

1 teaspoon Himalayan salt

Dash of cayenne

Bunch up the spinach, cilantro, and parsley, and push them through the hopper of a juicer with the carrots, apple, and celery. Pour into glasses, and stir in the salt and cayenne to taste.

Stomach Soother ....

Drink this often if you have digestive disorders or if you are on a juice cleanse or fast. Drink slowly.

7 ounces celery juice

3 ounces cabbage juice

1 ounce aloe vera juice

1 ounce parsley juice

½ ounce fennel juice

1 garlic clove

1 to 2 slices fresh ginger

Combine all the ingredients in a high-powered blender, and process until smooth.

Tomato Juice ....

4 to 5 very ripe tomatoes

1 to 2 cups water

½ teaspoon freshly squeezed lemon juice

Dash of cayenne

Combine all the ingredients in a high-powered blender, and process until smooth. Adjust the water to achieve the desired consistency. Chill thoroughly before serving.

Summer Cooler .... YIELD: 3 TO 4 SERVINGS

3 to 4 tomatoes

2 to 3 cucumbers

½ bell pepper (any color)

Dash of Flower of the Ocean sea minerals

Dash of freshly squeezed lemon juice

Parsley sprigs

Juice the tomatoes, cucumbers, and bell pepper in a masticating juicer. Pour into glasses, and add the sea minerals and lemon juice to taste. Mix well. Chill thoroughly before serving. Garnish with parsley sprigs.

Tomato Summer Quencher .... YIELD: 2 TO 3 SERVINGS

2 celery stalks

1 cucumber

2 to 3 very ripe heirloom tomatoes, chopped

½ teaspoon freshly squeezed lime juice

Put the celery and cucumber though the hopper of a juicer. Pour the juice into a high-powered blender. Add the tomatoes and lime juice, and process until well combined. Chill thoroughly before serving.

NOTE: Alternatively, chop all the vegetables, and place them in the a high-powered blender along with the lime juice and enough water to facilitate blending and achieve the desired consistency. Process until smooth. Chill thoroughly before serving.

Turnip Watercress Juice .... YIELD: 3 TO 4 SERVINGS

This juice is known as an aid for anemia and low blood pressure.

1 handful watercress

1 handful spinach leaves

1 handful turnip leaves

2 to 5 lettuce leaves

4 to 6 carrots

2 green apples

Push the watercress, spinach, turnip, and lettuce leaves through the hopper of a juicer with the carrots and apples. Serve immediately.

Watercress and Spinach Combo

YIELD: 2 TO 3 SERVINGS

This juice was recommended by Dr. Bernard Jensen to dissolve hemorrhoids and tumors.

1 handful turnip leaves

1 handful spinach

1 handful watercress

4 to 6 carrots

Push the turnip leaves, spinach, and watercress through the hopper of a juicer using the carrots. Serve immediately.

Athlete's Manna .... YIELD: 1 TO 2 SERVINGS

Use this to prepare for arduous hours of training and competition.

1 cup Hemp Milk (page 35)

¼ cup Incan berries

1 tablespoon E3Live

1 teaspoon spirulina

1 teaspoon dried mulberries

Combine all the ingredients in a high-powered blender, and process until smooth.

Vegetable Herb Delight .... YIELD: 4 TO 5 SERVINGS

1 zucchini

¼ cup coarsely chopped carrots

⅓ cup chopped celery (with leaves)

¼ cup coarsely chopped red bell pepper

1 handful fresh cilantro.

3 cups coarsely chopped tomatoes

¼ cup coarsely chopped onions

1 tablespoon chopped fresh basil

1½ teaspoons stevia powder or liquid

1½ teaspoons freshly squeezed lemon juice

1 teaspoon Celtic sea salt

1 teaspoon minced fresh sorrel

1 teaspoon minced fresh marjoram

1 small bay leaf

½ garlic clove

¼ teaspoon cayenne

Push the zucchini, carrots, celery, red bell pepper, and cilantro through the hopper of a juicer. Pour the juice into a high-powered blender. Add the remaining ingredients, and process on high until smooth. Add a small amount of water, if necessary, to facilitate blending and achieve the desired consistency. Serve at room temperature or thoroughly chilled.

Watercress Delight .... YIELD: 1 TO 2 SERVINGS

1 handful watercress

1 green apple

1 coconut, water and flesh

Juice the watercress and apple in a masticating juicer. Pour the coconut water into a high-powered blender. Scoop out the coconut flesh, and add it to the blender. Pour the juice into the blender, and process until smooth. Serve at once or thoroughly chilled.

NOTE: To retain the fiber, chop the apple and watercress, and place them in a high-powered blender with the coconut water and flesh. Process until smooth. Add a small amount of additional coconut water or water, if needed, to facilitate blending and achieve the desired consistency.

218   CELEBRATING OUR RAW NATURE

Vegetable Medley ....

2 carrots

2 apples

2 celery stalks

1 cucumber

½ cup fresh peas, still in pods or sprouted

¼ cup broccoli florets

¼ daikon

1 tablespoon Celtic sea salt

1 tablespoon freshly squeezed lemon juice

1 tablespoon raw hemp oil

1 cilantro sprig

1 slice fresh ginger

½ garlic clove

1 drop raw oregano oil

Dash of cayenne

Juice the carrots, apples, celery, cucumber, peas, broccoli, and daikon. Transfer the juice to a high-powered blender, add the remaining ingredients, and process until smooth and well blended. Adjust the salt and cayenne to taste.

Index

BOOK PUBLISHING COMPANY

since 1974—books that educate, inspire, and empower

To find your favorite vegetarian and soyfood products online, visit:
www.healthy-eating.com

Living in the Raw
Rose Lee Calabro
978-1-57067-148-7 $19.95

Living in the Raw Gourmet
Rose Lee Calabro
978-1-57067-176-0 $19.95

Angel Foods
Healthy Recipes for Heavenly Bodies
Cherie Soria
978-1-57067-156-2 $19.95

Raw Food Made Easy
Jennifer Cornbleet
978-1-57067-175-3 $16.95

Raw Food Made Easy DVD
Jennifer Cornbleet
978-1-57067-203-3 $19.95

Warming Up to Living Foods
Elysa Markowitz
978-1-57067-065-7 $15.95

Purchase these health titles and cookbooks from your local bookstore or
natural food store, or you can buy them directly from:

Book Publishing Company • P.O. Box 99 • Summertown, TN 38483
1-800-695-2241

Please include $3.95 per book for shipping and handling.